THE GREAT LIVES SERIES

Great Lives biographies shed an exciting new light on the many dynamic men and women whose actions, visions, and dedication to an ideal have influenced the course of history. Their ambitions, dreams, successes and failures, the controversies they faced and the obstacles they overcame are the true stories behind these distinguished world leaders, explorers, and great Americans.

Other biographies in the Great Lives Series

ACKNOWLEDGMENT

A special thanks to educators Dr. Frank Moretti, Ph.D., Associate Headmaster of the Dalton School in New York City; Dr. Paul Mattingly, Ph.D., Professor of History at New York University; and Barbara Smith, M.S., Assistant Superintendent of the Los Angeles Unified School District, for their contributions to the Great Lives Series.

THOMAS EDISON
INVENTING THE FUTURE

By Penny Mintz

FAWCETT COLUMBINE
NEW YORK

For middle-school readers

A Fawcett Columbine Book
Published by Ballantine Books

Produced by
The Jeffrey Weiss Group, Inc.
96 Morton Street
New York, New York 10014

Library of Congress Catalog Card Number: 89-90899

ISBN:0-449-90378-8

Cover design and illustration by Paul Davis

Manufactured in the United States of America

First Edition: February 1990

10 9 8 7 6 5 4 3 2

TABLE OF CONTENTS

1

The Machine Must Talk

I T WAS THE dead of night on December 3, 1877. Besides the shuffling of a few plow horses in their stalls, all was quiet in Menlo Park, New Jersey. The fields were empty; the houses and lanes were dark.

Only one pale light could be seen. It came from the second floor of a long wooden building, near the railroad station. Inside that building, gas lamps flickered all night long as three men worked feverishly. One of them was thirty-year-old Thomas Alva Edison, who was describing and sketching ideas he had for an astounding invention. He was trying to make a machine that could record speech.

Edison's ideas and thoughts tumbled out quickly, one on top of another. Luckily, Charles Batchelor, his chief assistant and partner, knew how to slow him down. As Edison's ideas flew out, Batchelor caught them and used them to draw up solid plans. By forcing Edison to follow each idea through, Batchelor was able to keep him on track.

Meanwhile, James Adams paced back and forth. Edison had hired Adams a few years earlier as a night watchman; but since Edison liked working at night, a guard wasn't really needed. Night after night, instead of being on the lookout for break-ins, Adams had watched Edison and Batchelor work. After a while, he had begun to make suggestions. Every so often, Adams stopped pacing, looked at a drawing, and made a comment. When he did, the other two men listened carefully. As often as not, the idea sounded good and they used it, pushing aside one drawing to begin another.

The hours passed quickly as Edison, Batchelor, and Adams bent over one of ten sturdy tables in the long, narrow room. All around them, tabletops were covered with books and notebooks, batteries, flasks, beakers, springs, magnets, tubes, and other bits and parts. Wires reached from the ceiling to measuring equipment: a galvanometer for measuring electric current, a photometer for measuring light, and an electrometer for measuring electric charge. The walls were lined with shelves holding hundreds of glass bottles filled with chemicals. This was the laboratory of Thomas Alva Edison.

At the time in America, homes were lit by kerosene lamps. People traveled from one place to another by horse-drawn carriage or railroad cars. There were no radio, movies, or television. No one — except Edison — had ever imagined that there would be such a miraculous thing as a phonograph. While people in the rest of the country were reading Mark Twain's newest book, *The Adventures of Tom Sawyer,* Edison and his assistants were busy at work in the world's first commercial laboratory — a factory built specifically to invent things. Edison believed in practical experiments, not theories. In his Menlo Park lab, he could experiment and test to his heart's content.

Edison's most important project at the moment was the telephone. Alexander Graham Bell had invented and patented the telephone a year earlier, in 1876, but people had to scream into his telephone in order to be heard. Even then, the gadget worked only over short distances. The Western Union telegraph company had hired Edison to come up with an improved model.

Edison, however, had so many ideas in his head that he was always working on more than one project at a time. Often, while working on one idea, he would realize that the principles he discovered, the new facts he had learned, could be applied to other inventions. In fact, it was while he was improving the telephone and the telegraph that he realized it was possible to create a talking machine. In November 1877, Edison had told the newspapers about his spectacular invention, the phonograph.

Edison boasted to the press that his invention would record great singers and entire symphony orchestras. Someday, he said, everyone would have one of his machines, along with 1,000 or more different recordings. Anytime they wanted, they would be able to listen to great music and hear readings of classic books without ever leaving home.

To a world that had no movies or electric lights, it may have seemed that Edison's imagination was running wild. To a certain extent, it was. All he had done, so far, was attach a pin to a thin metal disk. Then he had shouted "Halloo!!" at the disk while pulling a piece of waxed paper under the pin.

Edison knew that sound waves were strong enough to make the disk vibrate and move back and forth. Because of that vibration, the pin had left tiny marks on the waxed paper. When Edison ran the paper back under the pin, it set the disk vibrating once again. The result was an eerie, almost human sound. It was far from speech, but to Edison that made no difference. In his notebook Edison wrote, "There's no doubt that I shall be able to store up and reproduce automatically at any future time the human voice perfectly."

Edison knew he had hit on a significant principle, and he was sure he had the brains, and the laboratory, to work it out. He was going to make a talking machine, and he was not at all nervous about letting the world know about it before he actually worked out the details.

During the night of December 3-4, 1877, Edison, Batchelor, and Adams drew up three possible phonograph designs. In one, a coil of paper was pulled under a needle. Another had the needle resting on a grooved disk, which sat on a turntable. The third used a grooved cylinder that was turned with a hand crank.

By the time Edison sent Batchelor and Adams home to get some rest, the sun was already rising. Edison himself was too excited to sleep. He sat down to make a final drawing for his machinist. He decided to try the grooved-cylinder design first.

Whenever Edison worked, he focused completely on what he was doing. That morning, he barely noticed that the empty lab had once again filled with his assistants and that sunlight now streamed in the many eastern windows. Shutting off the gas lights, the men set to work.

Some of these men were trying to find out what

material would make the best diaphragm for the telephone. (A diaphragm is a thin, flexible disk that vibrates.) Others were working on telephone-speaker designs. Some were working on mimeograph machines and automatic telegraphs. All of them took orders directly from Edison.

The roar of the engines and the shriek of the saws coming from the machine shop hardly fazed Edison. He had been growing increasingly deaf ever since he was a child. The sawdust and metal shavings didn't bother him either. They certainly wouldn't mess up his clothes — he had been wearing the same suit for several days and would go a few more before he changed. He didn't even change when he went to sleep. Edison held the unusual belief that every time he changed his clothes, he changed his body chemistry, making it hard to fall asleep. Whenever he went home to bed, he dropped, fully clothed, straight onto his wife's clean sheets. All the smells and dirt of the lab and machine shop came right along with him.

When he finished the phonograph design, Edison took it downstairs to his machine shop. There, models were made of anything he wanted built, and then the finished models were brought back upstairs for testing. Edison never expected anything to work on the first try. Even if it did, he knew there would always be problems to iron out.

After handing the design to John Kruesi, his head machinist, Edison may have gone home to get some sleep, since he lived right down the road. But it's just as likely that he curled up behind the stairs or under a table in some quiet corner.

Later that day, Kruesi reported that the machine was

coming along fine, but Kruesi couldn't help wondering what it was supposed to do.

"The machine must talk," Edison replied.

"Talk!" Kruesi said, scratching his head, thinking that that seemed absurd. Kruesi looked at the machine, looked up at Edison, and then bet him two dollars that it wouldn't work. Two dollars was a good-sized bet in those days; most men had to work several hours to earn that much. But Kruesi thought the odds were in his favor. How could this thing ever talk? he thought. It was only a metal shaft and cylinder attached to a couple of diaphragms and tubes. A talking machine? Ridiculous!

It was evening before Kruesi finished and brought the new machine upstairs to Edison. There were still several men in the laboratory. They all looked at Edison's new device with interest, but nobody thought it would work. James Adams, who had been napping on a table, woke up, took one look, and bet a box of cigars against it. Edison himself had great doubts, but there was no going back now.

While everyone watched, Edison carefully wrapped a sheet of tinfoil around the cylinder. Tinfoil, he knew, was better than waxed paper for printing the movements of the needle. Once he had the tinfoil in place, he put his mouth near one of the disk-and-needle units. Then he turned the crank that turned the foil-wrapped cylinder, and shouted into the disk. "Mary had a little lamb," he said, "Its fleece was white as snow. And everywhere that Mary went, the lamb was sure to go."

When he was done, he put the needle back at the beginning of the cylinder. Then, slowly, he began to turn the hand crank. He heard nothing. He cranked a little faster. When he got the end, he dejectedly ran his hand through his hair. It hadn't worked. He hadn't heard a thing. Shaking his head in disappointment, he looked up at the others and found that they were all pale and wide-eyed.

Kruesi, who had grown up in the German-speaking part of Switzerland, was the first to speak. "Mein Gott in Himmel," he muttered, which means, "My God in Heaven."

After a few seconds, one man started clapping. The others joined him, clapping and then cheering. Before long they were all dancing around the room.

The phonograph was born. The sound had been higher pitched than Edison's own voice, and it was too faint for Edison's poor hearing to make out. But the machine had worked.

A few days later, Edison finally did change his suit. Then he tucked his phonograph under his arm and headed to the railroad station. He was on his way to New York City. After a steam-engine trip to the edge of the Hudson and a ferry ride across the river, Edison headed straight for the offices of the magazine *Scientific American*. He was ready to show the world.

The editor and writers at *Scientific American* all knew Thomas Edison. He was only thirty, but he was already an important inventor, and they had written several articles about his work. Just one month earlier they had run an article about Edison's idea of recording the human voice on a strip of paper. They must have thought that idea was mostly science fiction because they didn't know what to expect when Edison set his invention down on a desk.

Edison didn't keep them waiting. He cranked up the

machine, set the needle on the cylinder, and watched the writers and editors as they listened. The machine asked them, in Edison's voice, how they felt.

Where was this sound coming from, they demanded. Was Edison able to throw his voice? Was this some kind of trick?

The phonograph went on to say that it felt very well, thank you, before asking if the listeners liked the machine. The recording ended with a polite "Good night."

The assembled magazine staffers couldn't believe what they were seeing and hearing. They had Edison play the recording over and over. As he did, more and more people packed into the office. The crowd grew so large that after a while the editor was afraid the floor would collapse.

Edison's new invention delighted everyone. It could do such an amazing thing, and it was such an altogether new concept. Although he had been well-known in scientific circles before, once the newspapers started writing about the phonograph, Edison became truly famous. People everywhere began to believe there was nothing Thomas Edison couldn't do. All over the world, Edison began to be known as the "Wizard of Menlo Park."

"Are you a wizard?" a visitor to his laboratory at Menlo Park once asked.

"I don't believe in anything like that," Edison had said.

Edison's work wasn't magic. Instead, he soaked up information and scientific knowledge. He was clever and skillful and could see possibilities and solutions no one else saw. There was nothing quick about the way he worked, but he was a genius.

Edison spent weeks and months, sometimes years, testing and learning before he solved a problem. The phonograph was one of his few inventions to be developed quickly. Most of the things the Wizard of Menlo Park invented, such as the electric light bulb which would one day illuminate cities across the world, took so long to develop that many other people would have given up in frustration. Edison, though, took the positive view that each failure meant that he had eliminated one possibility, and that all he had to do was try it another way. No matter how long it took, once something caught Edison's interest, he wouldn't stop until he found the answer. Even as a boy, there was no end to the things he had to know about. Young Thomas Edison was the most curious child anyone had ever known.

2

The Child
Who Had to Know "Why?"

IN THE SMALL hours of February 11, 1847, Samuel Edison stood nervously by a window of his home in Milan, Ohio. He had built this sturdy brick house just a few years earlier. Its front rested atop a steep bank, and four white-shuttered windows faced a street that passed close to a white picket fence.

From the back window where he stood, Sam Edison usually had a wide view of the Huron Canal, which joined the Huron River and eventually fed into Lake Erie. But on this night, snow was falling so thickly that Sam could barely see the shingle mill he owned down by the water's edge. Not that he cared just then. Sam's thoughts were fixed on what was going on in the next room, where his wife, Nancy, was having a baby. After having borne four girls and two boys, Nancy was struggling with their seventh and last child.

At last the village doctor emerged from the bedroom. "You have another boy, Sam," said the worried-looking physician. There was nothing wrong with that news. So why did the doctor look so worried? Were Nancy and the new baby all right?

Nancy would be fine, the doctor assured Sam. But the baby was weak, even for a newborn, and his head was unusually large. This could mean trouble, the doctor told the concerned father. The baby might have brain fever, a swelling of brain tissue that is now called meningitis.

Such news would be nerve-racking for any parents, but it was particularly hard for the Edisons. They had already lost two young children, a girl and boy. Nancy Edison had taken the deaths hard. Though she had found comfort in religion, the thought of losing this new baby was too much to bear.

Fortunately, the doctor was partly mistaken. It was true that the baby was frail. He would always be coming down with one ailment or other, especially ear infections. His head was large, but, as it turned out, the only fever in little Thomas Alva Edison's brain was a fever to learn.

All children are curious about the world. All children ask questions. Young Al, as Thomas Alva Edison was called as a child, was no exception. But Al seemed unusually curious. His endless questions drove his father to exhaustion. "What makes the wind blow?" Al would ask. "How do birds fly?" "What makes the sky blue?"

Al's mother was more patient. Before her marriage, she had been a schoolteacher. She wanted a good education for all her children, but she especially wanted it for Al, who was being raised as if he was an only child. Only a few months after Thomas Alva was born, the

11

Edisons' three-year-old daughter, Eliza, had died. Al's two remaining sisters and one brother were almost grown up.

There was something unusual about Al. It was not just that he learned to walk and talk when he was especially young or that he asked so many questions. What made Al so unusual was that he always tested the answers that he got. From the beginning, he was an experimenter, an inclination that got him into trouble throughout his life.

His oldest sister, Marion, told a story about one of Al's earliest experiments, when he was only a toddler.

"Why is that goose squatting on those eggs?" Al had asked his mother.

Nancy explained that the goose was keeping the eggs warm.

"Why does she keep them warm?" he asked.

"To hatch them, my dear," she answered.

"What's 'hatch'?"

"It means letting the little geese come out of the shell. They are born that way."

"Does keeping the eggs warm make the geese come out?" the boy asked.

"That's right."

That afternoon, Al disappeared. When his mother looked out the window and didn't see him playing, she got nervous. When Al wasn't down near Sam's mill, where he liked to play with the scrap wood, she became frightened. After much calling and a panicked search, Al was finally found in a neighbor's barn, asleep on a nest. The little boy had put some goose eggs on a bed of straw and then squatted down to hatch them. The eggs probably would have hatched, too, had he only been left alone. Al couldn't understand why everyone had gotten so excited.

It was in another barn years later that an experiment got the six-year-old Al into much worse trouble. Al had always enjoyed watching the town blacksmith softening iron in his red-hot coals. He had also been fascinated with the candles and oil lamps his family burned at night. On a breezy day in the spring of 1853, he decided to see exactly how it was that fire worked.

In the cool, semidarkness of his father's barn, Al gathered some dry sticks, which he put in a neat little pile and lit. He wanted to see what would happen. What did happen should come as no surprise. In a wooden building full of straw, the fire quickly raged beyond the terrified boy's control. For a while, Al stamped on the flames and tried to put out the fire. But the smoke was so dense and the fire grew so big that soon he had to rush out of the barn to save his life.

In the meantime, other people had seen the smoke. Men came running over to help extinguish the flames. For a while, it looked as if the wind might carry the flames to Sam Edison's shingle mill. If that caught, with all its scrap wood and wood shavings, then the neighboring flour mill, grain-storage bins, brewery, blacksmith, and leather-tanner might also be in danger of catching fire. The entire waterfront was threatened.

Thick black smoke billowed out the barn door. Dozens of men, shouting orders to each other, formed a bucket brigade to bring water up from the canal to the fire. All the while, Al stood alone, whimpering, watching his father's barn burn to the ground. In the end the other buildings were saved, but the barn was completely lost.

It wasn't until the fire was under control that people turned to the skinny boy with the big wobbly head and asked him why he had started a fire in a barn? What was the matter with him? With his blue eyes brimming with tears, Al tried to explain. He had wanted to know how fire worked, he said. He just wanted to see.

The problem was, Sam Edison later said in somewhat raised tones, the boy had no sense. He always just wanted to see what would happen. He had just wanted to see what the inside of the grain elevator was like that time he fell in and almost suffocated in the wheat. Al fidgeted and got more and more upset as Sam continued. How can you teach a boy, Sam asked, who has no sense and refuses to obey? Hadn't he told the boy to stay away from Sam Winchester, that crazy town miller who was trying to build a hot-air balloon? He certainly had. But did Al listen? No. Time and again Sam found him over at Winchester's mill.

This time the crime was more serious — much more serious. This time, Sam decided, he would take a switch to his son right in the middle of the town square. The boy was becoming known as a troublemaker. Sam wanted to make an impression on him as well as on all the other children. No doubt the public punishment made an impression on Al, but it wasn't enough to keep him from further experimenting. Thomas Alva Edison had a lifetime of experimenting — and trouble — in front of him.

A year later, in 1854, the town of Milan saw the last of the mischievous Al. The shingle business was failing. The Edisons were moving on. In fact, the financial problems the Edisons faced were shared by nearly everyone in town. The cause was the steam engine. Railroad

14

tracks were being laid across the Midwest at that time, but the railroad had bypassed Milan.

By 1850 railroads were in every state east of the Mississippi River. To the Americans of the mid 1800s, the railroad was an incredible thing. It sped along at the death-defying rate of twenty miles per hour; on a straightaway it sometimes got up to twenty-five or thirty miles per hour. More than that, the railroads opened up new horizons. People could now easily travel from one town to another, and from one state to another. They were no longer isolated. Railroads also allowed goods to be sent more quickly from one town to another, and people started shipping their goods by trains instead of by ships or barges on the rivers or canals. Milan was a canal town. Without freight going through, business in Milan dropped off to a trickle.

It was a sad morning for the Edisons when Sam, Nancy, and the three children still living with them piled their belongings onto a wagon. The wagon carried them along the first leg of their journey, ten miles south to Norwalk, a village that had been wise enough to donate land for railroad tracks and was thriving as a result. From Norwalk, Al and his family climbed aboard the train to Toledo. Nancy may have been afraid the train would jump track, and been aching from sitting on the hard benches, but her youngest boy was not suffering. Seven-year-old Al was dancing with excitement.

Young Edison hadn't known anyone who had taken such a long journey on a train. He pressed his nose up against the window to watch the countryside fly by. When he got tired of that, he talked to the conductor or played in the aisle with his sister, Harriet, and brother, Pitt.

In Toledo, the Edisons were once again dependent on horses. A carriage took them north to Detroit, Michigan. From Detroit they boarded a paddle ship going up the St. Clair River. Leaning against the ship's rails, young Al was able to catch glimpses of the camp fires of Indian, or native American, villages. Native Americans were rarely seen in Milan, but up north, where there was still wilderness, Al watched native men in canoes following their ship a short way before disappearing into the thick brush along the riverbank.

The Edisons were on their way to Port Huron, Michigan, where a brother of Sam's lived. Port Huron was an active port town which, Sam had learned, was soon to be connected by rail to Detroit. In 1854, though, Port Huron was still a small settlement, surrounded by clean, nearly untouched woodlands and lakes. To the east and north were the vast waters of Lake Huron. To the south and west were thick forests.

Life was more rustic in Port Huron than it had been in Milan. There were fewer businesses. People were more dependent on the goods they produced on their own small farms. Many families still made their own candles and soap. Women wove cloth and then hand-sewed their family's clothing. The village did not yet have a public school. But it was here that Thomas Alva Edison, at seven years of age, would have his first brush with formal education.

The Edisons were barely settled into the big, wood-frame house that they had rented when Al became seriously ill with scarlet fever. This did not keep him from starting school in September 1855, but it may be part of the reason why he would always have trouble in class. The scarlet fever had infected his ears. Whenever fluid built up in his ears, it became very hard for him to hear. Still, he might have done fine had the teachers said anything that interested him.

The school Nancy Edison chose for her son was the one-room schoolhouse of the Reverend and Mrs. G.B. Engle. As in most schools of the time, the children learned by memorizing facts. Questions were not allowed. Al was used to running free and learning by exploring and testing. For the first time he had to sit still and learn things that he thought were stupid.

Al hated everything about the school. The Reverend, who carried a cane and used it to discipline children who displeased him, terrified Al. And Al, who was always letting his mind wander, often felt the bite of the Reverend's cane. The boy lasted until the cold weather began. The first time he stayed home with an ear infection, his mother decided to educate her child herself.

Nancy Edison taught Al by reading aloud and discussing great books. Together mother and son read books such as David Hume's *History of England* and Edward Gibbon's *History of the Decline and Fall of the Roman Empire*. At an age when most children could barely read, Al was enjoying William Shakespeare and Charles Dickens.

Nancy's teaching method turned out to be weak in grammar and math, but it had one great strength. When she saw talent, she was willing to give it free rein. That is exactly what happened when she gave her son a copy of R.G. Parker's *School of Natural Philosophy*. Parker's textbook listed basic scientific knowledge of the time and included experiments to prove those facts. Al loved reading history and literature, but science opened up a whole new world. This was exactly the kind of thing he had been trying to do with his experiments. He soaked up every bit of information in Parker's text and did every one of the experiments, even though it meant buying chemicals, flasks, wires, and other materials. Before long he had put together a small laboratory.

The laboratory started out in the middle of Nancy Edison's living room. But Nancy Edison could take just so much of the smells and spills of Al's experiments. Even worse were the experiments that ended up in small explosions or fires. Eventually, Nancy told her son to get his stuff out of the house. Al built shelves in the basement, labeled all his jars "poison," and took to experimenting downstairs.

Al did more than repeat the experiments of others in his basement laboratory. He had some ideas of his own. By 1857, for example, when he was ten years old, he had some creative ideas about flight.

Back in Milan, Al had loved to watch Sam Winchester, the town miller, as he tried to build a lighter-than-air balloon. Al noted that the balloon rose when Winchester filled it with gas. So, Al figured, all one had to do to make people fly was to fill them up with gas. Young Edison knew better than to experiment on himself. After all, he had to remain available for objective observation. Instead, he took a friend named Michael Oates down into his laboratory and talked him into being the "test pilot."

Al's plan was to give Michael several doses of Seidlitz powders, which were used to treat stomachaches. These powders, when mixed with water, bubbled up and gave off carbon dioxide. Edison figured that with all that gas inside him, Michael would simply float like a balloon.

Michael took the powders, but he never went up. He went down, straight to the floor, with unbearable stomach pain. As Al watched Michael groaning and twitching in the dirt, he quickly reached two related conclusions: Seidlitz powders wouldn't make people fly, but they could get a ten-year-old boy into big trouble.

In September 1857, Nancy Edison decided to give formal schooling another try. For a short while she enrolled Al in a private school, which he liked. Five months later, though, he was attending the two-story public school that had recently been built in Port Huron. Al was much happier at this school than he had been at the Engles's, but once again he began getting into trouble.

Part of the problem was that the children had to share books. Al was a much faster reader than the others; while they were still reading he grew bored. This may have been how he developed a taste for playing practical jokes, but because of the jokes, neither the teachers nor the students liked him very much. Sam Edison had a friend who suggested that Al's problems were caused by too much reading. According to his theory, reading overworked the boy's mind and left him all muddled up. The best thing Sam could do for his son, the man told Sam, would be to take Al out of school altogether.

Al's problem, however, lay not in being muddled. It was his ears. Ever since he was a baby, he had been prone to earaches. There were times when he could hear, but when his ears filled with fluid he had no idea what the teachers were saying. During the winter of 1859, Al became sick once again. The bones behind his ears became swollen, and he couldn't hear a thing.

19

Once again, his mother kept him out of school. This time, Thomas Alva Edison had left school for the last time. Train tracks had finally been laid between Detroit and Port Huron, and Sam Edison got his son a job on the railroad. Despite Nancy's objections that her boy was too young and that the work was too dangerous, twelve-year-old Thomas Edison went off to work.

3

The Candy Butcher

THOMAS EDISON LEFT the baggage car and opened the door to the train's wooden coach car. He stepped quickly inside and let the door slam behind him.

"Candy! Raisins!" he shouted. The passengers were sitting on benches against the walls of the car and staring out the windows or talking to each other.

"Magazines! Molasses! Figs!" he called. People looked up to see a thin, twelve-year-old boy with a big, wobbly head and thick, black hair pressed down under a cap. He was maneuvering his way carefully down the center aisle, hauling a heavy basket under one arm. With his other hand, he waved a couple of magazines.

Walking through the car was no easy task. The swaying movements of the train made it hard to keep one's balance, and Tom, as he now preferred to be called, dreaded the idea of being sent sprawling by a bump or lurch. Not only would that be embarrassing, but think of all the food! It would all be ruined, and he had already bought and paid for it.

Thomas Edison's job was as a candy butcher on the Grand Trunk Railroad. The job had nothing to do with butchering meat or even with cutting up candy. A candy butcher was someone who sold candy on a train. Tom also sold other foods, as well as tobacco, newspapers, and magazines. The railroad did not provide him with these items; he bought them with his own money. Whatever profit he made was his only pay. But that was okay because Tom saw money-making opportunities where no other candy butcher did. Over the next four years, he built up quite a business.

"Candy, mister? Peanuts?"

"Have you got any apples?"

"I'll bring you one my next time through."

Tom sold the dry foods first. This left people feeling thirsty, and so he ended up selling more fruit and drinks later. Tom had to be on the lookout for ways to make more money because his father couldn't get a business going in Port Huron. Tom's money was often the only regular income in the Edison household.

Tom worked hard to make extra money. His day started at six o'clock in the morning, when he bought produce and butter from the Port Huron farmers. Besides selling food to passengers, he also shipped and delivered fresh food — without paying freight charges. On the return train he would use that freight space to store Detroit newspapers, which he would sell along the way. He also had two boys running newsstands for him at stops along the line.

Free freight space had not been part of Tom's original agreement with the Grand Trunk Railroad. He had talked the conductor, Alexander Stephenson, into giving him that privilege. Tom was such a pleasant, hard-working boy, with bright eyes and a quick smile that Stephenson couldn't help but like him. Besides, Tom was a clever wheeler-dealer. He always gave Stephenson things, such as newspapers and cigars. It would have been hard to say no.

Tom's train left Port Huron at seven-fifteen in the morning and arrived in Detroit, sixty-three miles to the south, about four hours later. From then until half past six at night, when the return trip began, Edison was on his own. The layover time had been his mother's biggest worry. Detroit was a rough town for a twelve-year-old to be wandering around in all day.

Downtown Detroit spread out behind the wharves on the Detroit River. Since the Detroit River, in tandem with Lake St. Clair and the St. Clair River, links two of the Great Lakes — Erie and Huron — Detroit had become a major shipping center. Tom, still skinny and only partly grown, looked on wide-eyed at the loud, drunk, and often brawling sailors, ashore on a few hours' leave. He had never seen the likes of that back home on the streets of Port Huron.

Tom didn't spend much time at the waterfront, though. He had to buy the supplies he needed for the trip back. Once those chores were out of the way, he preferred the railroad yards or the city's machine shops or the downtown telegraph office to the wharves. What he liked best was to experiment, and the city made that possible.

Detroit, in 1859, was a center for chemical manufacturers. A young boy interested in science and walking around with change in his pocket could go to the shops and buy more chemicals and equipment than he had ever seen before. Over the months, Tom started accumulating chemicals, metal scraps, and tools. What he needed next was laboratory space. In 1860, Tom turned once again to Alexander Stephenson. There was still plenty of room in the baggage car, Edison pointed out. Could he use one corner as a lab?

With Stephenson's okay, Edison had four railed shelves built at one end of the car. Below the shelves he added a narrow wooden table and a trunk, for seating and storage. Thomas Edison spent every moment he could in this little lab: during the layover in Detroit and even while the train was rolling along, when he wasn't selling candy. Though the American political world was in turmoil — which in 1861 erupted into the Civil War — it was the physical world that held the most interest to Edison. He used that lab to start trying to figure out just how the physical world worked.

One lesson, learned the hard way, had to do with phosphorus. Phosphorus must be kept under water, because it ignites in air. One morning, while testing the truth of a fact he had read, Tom forgot that the water over his phosphorus was low. When the water evaporated, Tom's piece burst into flames, bounced out of the jar, and landed on the floor. The baggage room, which was full of newspapers, magazines, and burlap bags, provided perfect tinder.

Had Tom been less intent on what he was doing, he might have been able to get that phosphorus back into some water and stamp out the fire. But it took him a while to notice. Even without the noise of the train's wheels on the rails, he couldn't hear the crackling of the fire, and he ignored the smell of smoke. Smoke was always coming in from the engine's smokestack. By the time Tom finally turned around, the flames were eating away at his papers and spreading to the wooden floor of the car itself. Horror-stricken, he jumped up and began a frenzied and fruitless effort to swat out the flames.

Luckily, Conductor Stephenson saw the fire from the next car. He rushed in to throw water on it, and the two of them worked side-by-side until the only flame was the still-burning phosphorus. The conductor, not knowing what it was, picked it up to throw it out. To his horror, the chunk stuck to his fingers, burning them and adding considerably to the barrel of trouble that Tom was already in. When the train pulled in at Mount Clemens, the next stop, Tom watched, numb with misery, as Stephenson took everything in the lab and threw it off the train.

Alexander Stevenson got so angry that day that, legend has it, he punched young Tom in the ears, supposedly causing his deafness. Edison later said that story was untrue, and that his deafness began earlier. One day, Edison claimed, this same conductor saved his life by grabbing him by the ears and pulling him up into a moving car.

"I was trying to climb into the freight car with both arms full of papers when the conductor took me by the ears and lifted me," Edison said. "I felt something snap inside my head, and my deafness started from that time and has ever since progressed."

Doctors doubt that this is what caused Edison's permanent deafness. Rather, they believe the snap was the sound of Tom's outside ear as it broke away from his skull. Fluid in his ear then pressed up against his eardrum, cutting off his hearing temporarily. The long-term deafness, they said, was more likely caused by

Tom's bout with scarlet fever in 1854, followed by years of untreated ear infections.

Thomas Edison may have been one of the most successful candy butchers of all times, but right from the beginning he was on the lookout for a better job. There wasn't enough profit in candy; he wanted a real career.

Like most boys in those days, one of Tom's dreams was to become a train engineer. In his eyes, the engineer was just about the most impressive person in the world. Tom would do anything — lug water, polish brass fittings — for him. One day Tom got the chance of a lifetime. The engineer and the fireman, whose main job was to feed fuel to the engine, had both come to work after a late night out and wanted to do nothing but sleep. Tom assured them that since he had been watching them for months he could drive the train.

Everything started out just fine. Tom brought the speed down to twelve miles an hour, just to be safe, and he never once forgot that the steam engine needed water.

"I knew," Edison said later, "that if it got low, the boiler was likely to explode." So he kept adding water, plenty of water — a little too much water, it turned out. He added so much water that it passed into the smokestack and was forced out, carrying all the accumulated soot with it.

"I hadn't gone twenty miles before black, damp mud blew out of the stack," Edison recalled. It must have been a long, dreadful instant when Tom first saw the black muck that would soon drench him and the engine. In those days, railroad workers took great pride in keeping their engines well shined and polished. What would they say? What would they do?

The next station was in sight. Whenever the train came to a station, the fireman always climbed out onto the cowcatcher in the front of the train to add oil to the engine. The train might have been a mess, but Tom was determined to get this task done right. What he had failed to notice was that the engineer always turned the steam off before the fireman opened the oil cap. As soon as Tom twisted the cap, a blast of steam blew out, nearly knocking him off the engine. He grabbed the cowcatcher and just managed to hold on. Still, it was clear to the people gathered at the station that the young Edison boy, covered with greasy muck and riding into town grappling with a cowcatcher, did not have the stuff of which train engineers were made.

Since engineering was out, it was a good thing Tom had another interest: the news. A few weeks before his fifteenth birthday in 1862, he was wandering around the shops of Detroit when he saw a secondhand printing press and 300 pounds of type for sale. Why not sell his own newspaper? he thought. He made so little profit on the papers he was selling. Surely he could do better publishing his own.

Once more Tom turned to Alexander Stephenson for space in the baggage car. Once more Stephenson gave his okay. A newspaper press sounded a lot safer than a chemistry lab. In 1862, Edison began publishing his own newspaper, the *Grand Trunk Weekly Herald*.

Much of Edison's paper was taken up with information about schedules, fares, and stagecoaches that met the train. Food prices at the market were listed. Ducks were thirty cents a pair on February 3, 1862. Eggs were twelve cents a dozen. From telegraph operators at the railroad stations, Edison learned war news. The Civil

27

War was raging in 1862, and people wanted to read about it.

Edison printed about 400 copies of each *Weekly Herald*. He charged three cents a copy and eight cents for a one-month subscription. But when he got started, he had no idea how hard it was to put out a newspaper. After gathering the news items and writing them up, Tom still had to spend many hours bending over the lines of type, searching for each letter, and jamming it in place. His back ached. The winter winds buffeted the unheated baggage car. But he couldn't stop; he had too much to do. Once the letters and the lines fit the columns, he still had to press out each of the 400 copies by hand.

After a few issues of the *Weekly Herald*, Edison had another idea. He knew a boy, named Will Wright, who worked in a printer's shop. Tom talked Will into being his partner on a new publishing venture. Wright would print. Edison would write. They would call the paper *Paul Pry*, and it would be full of gossip and society news.

Paul Pry was also short-lived. The paper folded when a doctor in town got angry about an item he had read, came looking for Edison, found him down by the town docks, and pitched him into the river. That quenched Tom's interest in publishing.

Though his own newspaper did not bring Tom the fortune he sought, it was in the newspaper business that Edison made his first killing. On April 6, 1862, Tom made more money selling papers than he ever imagined possible.

Tom had noticed that on the days when big news stories broke — such as the day the Confederate, or Southern, troops fired on the Northern forces at Fort

Sumter and started the Civil War, or the day the Southern forces overwhelmed the Union Army, the Northerners, at Bull Run — people gathered at the telegraph offices, hungry for information. At these times, he sold many more papers than usual.

April 6, 1862, was one of those big-news days. The crowds were so thick outside the offices of the Detroit *Free Press* that Tom had to push his way inside to pick up the papers he would sell on the train. News of the Battle of Shiloh, which was being fought in Tennessee, had broken. Families in the Detroit area had sons in that battle, and word was out that the Northern losses were heavy.

On an average day, Tom bought between 100 and 200 newspapers. On this April day he had enough money to buy 300, but with all the interest he saw in the news, he wanted 1,000 copies.

The frazzled office manager pushed aside the poorly dressed candy butcher who had worked his way through the crowds of people, all of them pleading for the names of the wounded and dead. He had no time to listen to Tom trying to explain why he should get an extra 700 copies of the paper on credit. But Tom wouldn't take "no" for an answer. He pressed on past and walked in on Wilbur Storey, the newspaper's editor.

It was quieter in the editor's office, but Tom had to talk fast. Before Storey had a chance to work himself into a fit over the nerve of this boy barging into his office, Tom had to get the man to understand why he thought he could sell 1,000 newspapers in one day. Tom's plan was to let people in neighboring towns know that there was big news by wiring it to the telegraph operators all along his route. The operators would then post the headline on each station's bulletin board. When the train stopped in each town, Tom would sell the newspapers on the platform.

Why, Storey may have wondered, would the telegraphers do that for Edison? Because he was friendly with them. Edison had always liked talking to the telegraphers, watching them sending and receiving messages and being the first to get the news that came over the wire. They, in turn, had been happy to have Tom around, even though he made them answer a lot of foolish questions about how things worked. Besides, he was always generous with cigars and papers.

Tom had 1,000 newspapers neatly folded and stacked in the baggage car when the train pulled into Utica, its first stop. Tom usually sold two papers at Utica, but there was a crowd at the station that day. At first, Edison thought they were all going on some kind of group trip. They weren't. It was the news posted by the telegraphers that brought them, as Tom realized when they all rushed over and surrounded him the moment he stepped off the train. He sold 35 newspapers at Utica.

When he saw a crowd at Mount Clemens, where he usually sold six or eight papers, he raised the price of the paper from five cents to ten. By the time he got to Port Huron, he was calling out, "Twenty-five cents apiece, gentlemen! I haven't enough to go around." Edison sold all 1,000 copies of the paper that day, and went home with his pockets bulging with money.

"Then I realized that the telegraph was a great invention," Edison said later. He decided, right then and there, that what he wanted to do was to become a telegraph operator.

4

Telegrapher for Hire

REMEMBERING HOW HE had sold those 1,000 newspapers, Edison said years later, "It was the notices on the bulletin board that had done the trick. I determined at once to become a telegrapher."

The telegraph would play a key role in Edison's life, not just in relation to his work as a telegrapher, but because Edison would use the fundamental scientific knowledge that was the basis of the telegraph to come up with many of his most significant inventions.

The telegraph, like the train, had revolutionized America. In fact, the two were linked. It was the telegraph that made train travel safe. Via the telegraph, stationmasters reported the arrivals and departures of the trains to the stationmaster down the line. If an expected train didn't arrive on time, then there was a good chance it was stalled somewhere. Because the stationmaster could wire that news to the other stations and prevent any other trains from coming down the tracks, many accidents were avoided.

The way a telegraph worked was very straightfor-

31

ward. Each time the telegraph key was pressed down, an electric circuit was completed. This allowed a small burst of current to run through a wire to a sounder at the other end. At the receiving end, the current flowed through an electromagnet — a coil of wire wrapped around an iron core — and the electromagnetic force pulled down the sounder, an iron bar, with a click. At the end of the signal the key was lifted, the current stopped, and a spring snapped the sounder up with another click.

Samuel F.B. Morse, who had invented the telegraph in 1837, turned his invention into something useful by developing a code. In Morse code, every letter and number has its own combination of short and long signals, the lag time between clicks. These are called dots and dashes. By 1861, a transcontinental telegraph line had been completed, meaning that across America, people were able to send messages much faster than they ever could with their previous method, the pony express. Now, information could travel as fast as electricity.

Edison's determination was not something to be taken lightly. When he had wanted to be a train engineer, his dream had come true, if somewhat imperfectly. When he had decided to be a newsman, he had published his own paper. But now that he had determined to be a telegraph operator, there were problems to overcome. He couldn't simply go out and get a job; he had to learn how to work the telegraph key. But first he had to have a key to work.

By spending his free time haunting Detroit's machine shops and equipment stalls, Tom was able to gather the materials he needed to make his own telegraph set. Then he built a set like the one he had read about in a magazine. He and his neighbor Jim Clancy climbed trees and squeezed through bushes to string wire between their houses. Every night, when Edison came home from work, they spent hours slowly, laboriously, clicking messages back and forth. Neither of them was very good at taking Morse code, but Tom had more patience than Jim. Whenever Jim had trouble figuring out what Tom had sent, he would go out in his yard, climb up the back fence, and call out for help. This made Tom so angry his eyes would bulge.

Tom and Jim kept up their nightly practicing until a stray cow got caught in their wire one day and ripped it down. But in January 1863, a few weeks before his sixteenth birthday, Tom began a more serious study of telegraphy. Sam Edison had gone over to Mount Clemens to have a talk with James Mackenzie, a friend of the family and the telegrapher at the Mount Clemens station. Mackenzie agreed to take Tom on as a telegraphy student.

The winter winds shook the small railroad tank house where Tom sat with his telegraph key, concentrating hard and learning fast. He and another telegraph student, sitting 100 feet away in the station house, tapped out Morse code messages to each other under the watchful eye of James Mackenzie, the twenty-five-year-old stationmaster.

"M-I-S-S-I-S-S-I-P-P-I. Mississippi!"

Tom did it. He had gotten it off. Mississippi was the first long word Tom learned to send on the telegraph. He was on his way.

Edison spent the first five months of 1863 candy butchering his way every morning from Port Huron to

Mount Clemens. From then until the return train arrived, he practiced telegraphy and learned its shortcuts. For those five months, Edison was totally absorbed. For once there was no time in his life for experimenting — and the trouble that usually resulted.

Tom's first telegraph job came during the summer of 1863. Even before he knew how to decode by ear — without first seeing the dots and dashes written out — Tom got a part-time job in the quiet Port Huron jewelry shop that doubled as the town's telegraph office.

From the beginning, it was clear that telegraphy had been a good choice. For one thing, despite his increasing deafness, Tom could hear the clicks of the key. He claimed he could hear them better than most people, because background noises never distracted him. The voices of children playing in the street, the clattering of horse-drawn wagons, the conversations about the weather between the jeweler and his friends — those were the kinds of sounds that Tom had trouble hearing.

For another thing, Tom loved the telegraph itself. He liked puttering around with it, trying to improve it. He also liked mixing the chemicals for the batteries that gave the telegraph its power. Finally, his new job left him plenty of free time. Between the few messages going in and out of Port Huron, he was able to read and, even better, experiment. Most of his experiments involved testing the truth of the facts he read. He trusted none of the work of others — and never would.

Trouble started up again over the jeweler's tools. Thomas Walker expected to find his tools as he had left them — in the same place and the same condition — but Tom kept borrowing them and, like most sixteen-year-old boys, he never remembered to return anything. Worse still, if he happened to expose a delicate instrument to harsh chemicals or ruin it by using it to cut wires, Tom didn't care. That never seemed as important to him as doing his experiment.

Despite Tom's annoying treatment of the tools, Walker kept Edison on — at least, that is, until the explosion. One fine fall day, while the jeweler was up by the big front window, using the daylight to work, Edison was out back with a couple of friends, showing them how he mixed the chemicals for the batteries. He put in a little of this and a little of that. He had often improvised. On that day — his last as the Port Huron telegrapher — the mixture blew.

After the dust settled, Tom found a job up north, in Canada. The Grand Trunk Railroad hired him to work the night shift in its Stratford Junction office. There, in a small, bare office, Edison worked in the dim light of a kerosene lamp. He had nothing but the noise of the crickets to keep him company, and because his hearing was so poor, Tom felt very much alone.

The work itself was easy. One or two messages about train schedules came over the line, and every once in while a train had to be signaled. There was one other small chore. Every hour, the signal for the number six had to be sent out. That was how the manager made sure his night telegraphers were awake. Night after night, from 7 P.M. to 7 A.M., Tom had nothing to do but read and wait for the next hour to "six" the line. As he sat, the need for sleep would press in on him. Most days, he had spent the morning reading the town's three newspapers and the afternoon working on experiments. He was tired. All that kept him from getting a good rest was that hourly need of "sixing." Surely there was something he could rig up to do that simple job for him.

What he did was hook up a clock that kicked a switch every hour on the hour. Whenever that switch was pulled, the telegraph was rigged to send out the "six." It was Thomas Edison's first useful invention. For the first time, Edison had used his knowledge to invent a better way of doing something rather than just verifying the findings of others, and he liked the feeling of accomplishment it gave him.

However, the Grand Trunk Railroad was not pleased. One night, while he was asleep, the main office sent him some follow-up messages. Unfortunately, he had not devised an invention to answer those. He got away with a stern warning, but if he got into trouble again, he was told, he would be fired.

That fate befell him when he failed to signal a train one night. Edison had received a message to hold a train and had immediately telegraphed back that he would. However, as he went out to tell the signalman, the train sped past.

"I ran to the telegraph office and reported that I could not hold her," Edison later said.

The train dispatcher responded with a curse. Edison was smart enough to figure out that the dispatcher had already allowed a train to leave the next station. The two trains were heading straight toward each other. Sick with fear, Tom tried to run through a gully to catch the train before it rounded a bend. He never got there. In the dark, he hit his head on a low branch and was knocked out. Fortunately, the trains' engineers saw each other's lights and were able to stop their trains in time.

Once again Tom was called into the manager's office. This time, as Tom sat fidgeting, the manager slammed his fist into his desk and threatened to send the boy to jail. It's possible that the man was only trying to scare him, but Tom didn't stick around to find out. While the manager was called away, Tom sneaked out and ran — without stopping to ask for the $28 he was owed in wages. He kept going until he was safely across the Canadian border and back in the United States.

Tom was seventeen years old, old enough to be considered an adult. From then on he would work in cities far from home. Over the next few years he moved frequently, going from one telegraph job to another. From 1864 until the Civil War ended in April of 1865, there was always another telegraph job to be had. Every town, every railroad stop, needed telegraphers. The army kept drafting them away, and telegraph companies were so desperate they would take anyone.

Tom Edison, though, managed to get fired as regularly as he was hired. Sometimes it was because of a practical joke he had played, such as giving people electric shocks by hot-wiring a telegraph key. Other times he was caught sleeping at work. Sometimes something would blow up during his experimenting — he often used company time to invent things, such as pest-killers that electrocuted roaches or rats with a loud zap when they stepped on two small metal plates to close an electric circuit. Even though inventing was still getting him in trouble, nothing would stop him. By late 1864, inventing had become more important to Edison than being a telegrapher.

While working in Indianapolis, Indiana, in the fall of

1864, Edison again put his inventiveness to practical use. He wanted to be able to take messages straight off the clicking sounder instead of relying on reading the dots and dashes on paper. If he did so he could move up from plug, or beginner operator, to first-class operator. But the dots and dashes came too fast, making it all sound like a blur. In order to practice building up speed, he altered some old telegraph machines, which wrote out the dots and dashes in pencil. He had one machine make small holes in a roll of paper instead of pencil marks, and he had the other turn those holes back into clicks. By hooking them up with a timer in the middle, Edison created a repeater that could replay the messages at any speed he wanted.

After several lectures about the time he was wasting on inventions instead of doing his work, Edison left Indianapolis for Cincinnati, Ohio. He was working there on April 14, 1865, the night the telegraph wires brought the news that President Abraham Lincoln had been assassinated.

In Memphis, Tennessee, Edison developed an automatic repeater that made a significant improvement to telegraph service. Over long distances, the strength of the electric signals became too weak to receive. To make up for this flaw, a message that was being sent long distance had to be taken down and then sent out again by several telegraph receivers along the route. Now, instead of human beings receiving and sending out messages, this work could be performed by Edison's automatic repeater.

Unfortunately, Edison's boss had been working on the same problem. After beating his boss to it, Edison was accused of being a troublemaker and was once again out of a job. Even though he had been making first-class operator pay, he was also flat broke; he never had been one to save. On one payday he had begged other telegraphers to lend him money for food, since he had already spent it on books and equipment. Clothes had even less priority for him than food. When Edison left Memphis during the winter of 1866, he was jobless, penniless, and clothed in a duster, a thin jacket designed to keep dust off rather than warmth in.

By 1866, the South that Edison traveled through was a wild, dangerous place. The Civil War was over, but the South was in a state of disarray. Plantations, farms, towns, and cities had been destroyed, collapsing the economy. New local and state governments had to be re-established in order for the Southern states to be readmitted to the Union. But first they had to meet the many and oftentimes conflicting requirements of the Northern political officeholders. It was several years before many of the southern states would once again have local governments. Meanwhile, gunfighters ruled the streets, and saloons were open all night. In one town a church doubled as a gambling hall. Making his way through this chaos, Edison walked and hitched rides on trains and eventually reached Louisville, Kentucky.

Louisville had a telegraph office that was typical of the day. Located on the second floor of a worn-out wooden building, the place was filthy. Rats ran around brazenly, scampering through the garbage and the piles of books and messages. The telegraph machines were set up on tables crowded all around the room. Since each machine had to be attached to a central switchboard, there were masses of wires running over tables, up to the ceiling, over to the switchboard, out the door, and into the battery room.

Into this office one bitter cold day in 1866 walked eighteen-year-old Thomas Edison. His clothes were frayed and wrinkled, and it had been weeks since he had taken a bath. As he leaned up against a wall, skinny and dirty, waiting to see if he would get a job, he chewed a wad of tobacco and spit. He didn't say much, but when he spoke, it was with a country twang. Though he looked like a tramp, his appearance and life-style were actually so typical of the kind of telegraphers who moved around from job to job that some said he should be dipped in bronze and saved for posterity.

Edison was different, though. He may have lived on a cot in the hall of a boardinghouse, but unlike other tramp telegraphers, his space was filled with books and science equipment. While the others relaxed and enjoyed themselves after work, Edison spent his time reading. When his shift ended at three o'clock in the morning, the first thing Edison did was buy all the local newspapers so that he could read them over his breakfast of coffee and pie. After breakfast he returned to his cot in the hall and got down to the business of educating himself. In the process, Edison more than made up for his lack of formal schooling. He read everything he could on every subject that interested him. Sitting on the floor and leaning up against his cot, Edison bit off a chunk of tobacco and then picked up the books and journals one by one. He stopped only to try something out or to test one of his ideas.

Edison didn't want to waste any more time on telegraphy jobs. All he wanted to do was invent. Still, he had to support himself somehow. What he needed, he figured, was a blockbuster invention, such as the duplex, a machine several telegraphers around the country were trying to develop. A duplex could send two messages over one telegraph wire at the same time, doubling the traffic and profits that one wire could bear. Western Union, which by 1866 had grown into the biggest telegraph company in the United States, was willing to pay a great deal of money for such an invention. Edison wanted to be the one to come up with it.

By late 1866, toward the end of his stay in the Louisville office, Edison was letting telegraph messages pile up while he used the company wires to test his ideas for the duplex. Instead of going home after work, he went to a machine shop that was located behind the office. He spent nearly all day in that shop, taking telegraph machines apart and putting them back together. Beside him, workers yelled at each other, carriages under repair collapsed with crashes, and the hammering of metal on metal rang out. Edison never looked up. All he thought about was getting one wire to run two messages. All he saw was the problem before him.

Sometimes he was so still and quiet in the midst of the bustle of the shop that it looked as if he was asleep. He wasn't. He was thinking. As soon as he came up with an idea, he was all movement, grabbing tools he needed or jumping up to string wires from the machine shop to the telegraph office so that he could run a test. In fact, he made a general nuisance of himself trying to create a duplex.

By the beginning of the new year, 1867, Edison, twenty years old, had left Louisville for Boston, Massachusetts, where a friend named Milton Adams told him there was a job available. Based on Adams's recommendation, Edison came north to a city full of small machine shops run by inventors who were busy constructing, improving, and coming up with new machines. Edison didn't know it at the time, but he had. gotten himself to the right place at the right time. In. Boston, Thomas Edison's life would take a new turn.

5

Full-Time Inventor

THE WELL-DRESSED gentlemen who worked in Boston's Western Union office were not much impressed with Thomas Edison when he arrived in the spring of 1867. He looked like a field hand, with a frayed blue-flannel shirt and jeans high above his ankles. He wore a torn straw hat and was chewing a wad of tobacco, stopping only to spit. When he was hired, the other telegraphers decided to put this country bumpkin to the test. He was asked to take a special report for the Boston *Herald*. Unknown to Edison, one of New York's fastest senders was standing by, ready to work Edison over.

The New York dispatcher started out slowly. As he began to pick up speed, Edison glanced up for an instant and noticed that the other operators were unusually interested in how he was doing. He knew then, he said, that they "were trying to put up a job on me." He said nothing.

The New York dispatcher began to speed up. When the dispatcher was sending as fast as he could, he slurred over some words and ran the signals together. Still Edison stayed with him.

"I was used to this style of telegraphy in taking report, and was not in the least discomfited," Edison recalled. "Finally, when I thought the fun had gone far enough . . . I quietly opened the key and remarked, telegraphically, to my New York friend, 'Say, young man, change off and send with your other foot.'"

The Boston telegraphers burst into laughter. Here was a fellow the others could appreciate. Despite the clothes and the chewing tobacco, they liked Edison — for now. Eventually they, too, would grow tired of his practical jokes. But for now, he had a place.

Edison found his real home, however, in the company of other inventors in Boston's numerous workshops. In the 1860s the United States was in the midst of a great change — from a nation of farmers to an industrial society, utilizing power-driven machinery to produce goods. The machine shops of Boston were bubbling and percolating and spewing out many of the inventions that industry needed. Edison thrived in this atmosphere. He loved being around people who understood what he was doing and talked to him about their own work. He loved seeing inventions taking form under the greasy, screeching, metal-spitting machines. He loved the excitement of being part of America's Industrial Revolution.

"I am now twenty-one," he told his roommate, Milton Adams, less than a year after arriving in Boston. "I have got so much to do and life is so short. I am going to hustle."

The work that most interested Edison was the telegraph. He didn't much like operating it, but he did like making it more useful. In October 1868, he applied for his first patent, for an invention based on the telegraph — a machine that would telegraph lawmakers' votes quickly and automatically. A patent gives an inventor ownership rights. Once granted, the inventor is the only one who can manufacture or use the invention without special permission. Edison would eventually be the owner of 1,093 patents, more than any other inventor.

Edison also became an independent businessman in 1868 — not a rich one, just an independent one. He set up a business that telegraphed changes in the price of gold. For months, Tom and a partner spent days scrambling over Boston's rooftops adding wires to a maze of telegraph wires already thick enough to throw deep shadows on the streets below. They were connecting clients to a transmitter at the Boston gold exchange.

In the meantime, Tom was still working nights. He was hardly producing work that made Western Union proud. Rather, those nights were spent mostly sleeping or testing new ideas. In January 1869, a few weeks before his twenty-second birthday, that luxury came to an end. As a lark, he had written a 2,000-word report on a single sheet of paper, in letters so tiny that they could only be read under a magnifying glass. Because his boss complained, Edison wrote his next report so big that it wasted several pounds of paper. The boss was not amused, and Edison was again out of a job.

A day after being fired, Edison showed up at the offices of a telegraph journal, a magazine of industry news and advertisements. He had a notice to publish: "Thomas A. Edison would hereafter devote his full time to bringing out his inventions."

He needed income. He was drawing every cent he

could from the gold-ticker business, but that business earned barely enough to keep its lines in order. To make more money, the business needed a more reliable printer. But how could he pay the costs of developing that printer or, more important to Edison, afford to work on his duplex?

In June 1869, desperate for cash, Edison learned that he had been granted his patent for the automatic vote-counter. If he could just sell the machine to a few government legislatures, he thought, his problems would be solved. Patent in hand, Edison went to the Massachusetts legislature and to the U.S. Congress. Unfortunately, both Boston and Washington taught Edison a sad truth. Efficiency was the last thing lawmakers wanted. They wanted the process of voting to take a long time, so that the minority side could take the floor and talk endlessly, thus holding up or postponing the vote through a process called the filibuster.

Edison said he did "a heap of thinking" and came to a major decision on his way home from Washington, D.C. "I decided that if I wanted to be a free-lance inventor — and also eat on occasion — I was going to have to stick to inventing things that were sure to be in commercial demand." Never again would Edison work on anything unless he was sure it would sell. He couldn't afford to be a research scientist, who tries to answer questions without worrying about possible commercial use. He had to be an applied scientist, working not only toward making useful things but also things that people wanted.

Edison had been counting on making money with that vote-recorder. He had recently borrowed $800 to run a test to prove that the duplex would work over a long distance, between Rochester and New York City. Eight hundred dollars was a small fortune in 1869, when skilled workers earned thirty cents an hour. When the test failed, he was in big trouble. He had no income, he couldn't meet his expenses or pay his debts, and no one in Boston would lend him a cent. Down to his last couple of dollars, Tom decided to blow it all on a steamship ticket to New York City. He was gambling on finding fresh financing in the bigger city.

On a sparkling summer morning in 1869, Edison's steamship threaded its way through the heavy traffic on the Hudson River to land on New York's West Side. Edison walked off the wooden pier into the middle of one of the busiest markets in one of the busiest cities of the world. Vendors, yelling above the clanging and screeching of the trolley cars, called out the prices of their fruits and vegetables, meats and fish. Crowds of people jostled Tom as they threaded their way through the shops and stalls and around the streets. Everyone stepped gingerly, especially the women in their long, full skirts. They were trying to avoid the large mounds of horse droppings that were everywhere on the cobblestoned streets. Meanwhile, horses and carts clattered noisily right through these mounds, splattering the offensive-smelling mess.

The roar of the city made no difference to Edison. His deafness protected him. Edison often said he was glad for that protection — it saved his nerves. But deafness could not protect him from the rumbling in his stomach. He was hungry and, as usual, he was broke.

It took Edison the better part of his first day in New York to find a telegrapher willing to lend him some money: one dollar. Even in 1869, one dollar wouldn't last long. With that one dollar, he went into a restaurant and carefully studied the menu before finally settling on coffee and apple dumplings. It was the cheapest meal he could get, but to the famished twenty-two-year-old it tasted wonderful. For the rest of his life, Edison spoke of that meal as one of his most delicious. Dumplings and pies would always be among his favorite foods.

Edison couldn't talk anyone into refinancing his Boston business. But he did get some personal help from Franklin Pope, an employee of Samuel S. Laws, the inventor of the gold-ticker. Pope, a well-known telegraph expert, had been very impressed with Edison when they had met in Boston. Pope was now the foreman of Laws's company, Gold Indicator. He gave Edison a few repair jobs and told Edison he could bed down on a cot in the company's battery room. That was why Edison was around three days later, when a transmitter broke and work at Gold Indicator ground to a halt. It was to be Edison's lucky break.

"Within two minutes over 300 boys — a boy from every broker in the street — rushed upstairs and crowded the long aisle and office," Edison recalled. "It was pandemonium." Everyone was pushing and yelling, trying to get gold prices.

Franklin Pope was away at the time, so Edison looked to see what had gone wrong. Laws appeared on the scene and demanded to know what had happened. While his employees stood before him, terrified and dumbstruck, Edison spoke up. As calmly as possible, he said that he had found the problem.

"Fix it! Fix it! Be quick," Laws yelled above the uproar of 300 messengers fighting for gold prices.

48

Edison fixed the machine, but it took several hours to get the system going again because every receiver had to be reset. As Edison worked, Laws kept running nervously over, pressuring Edison to hurry. Finally, Edison mentioned that he could make a device that would keep all the receivers running in unison so that they would never have to be adjusted again. Laws stopped in his tracks. He immediately offered Edison a job if he would work on such a device. They later agreed on $225 a month.

"This was such a violent jump from anything I had ever had before that it rather paralyzed me for a while," Edison recalled. "I thought it was too much to be lasting; but I determined to try and live up to that salary if twenty hours a day of hard work would do it."

He was right — the job didn't last, but not because of anything Edison did wrong. Two months after Edison was hired, Samuel Laws sold the company to his main competitor, the Gold & Stock Telegraph Company. After the sale, Gold Indicator Company was dissolved. Edison did some work for Gold & Stock, but by mid-September he was unemployed again. This time, however, the prospect of starvation was less threatening. Now, he knew people.

On October 1, 1869, Thomas Edison, twenty-two years old, opened a workshop in Jersey City, New Jersey. His main partner was Franklin Pope, the foreman from Laws's gold-ticker company. Pope was to run the business end of the company; Edison was to concentrate on inventing and improving stock-tickers and transmitting equipment. Pope, Edison & Company planned to compete with Gold & Stock.

Edison had finally become a full-time inventor. There

was just one flaw in this otherwise perfect picture. He had always wanted to be a *rich,* full-time inventor, not to live luxuriously but to be able to afford all the time, space, equipment, and help he wanted for experimenting and inventing.

The business Edison started with Pope was never much of a competitor for Gold & Stock, but it did own some valuable patents, patents that Gold & Stock wanted. In 1870, Pope, Edison & Company was merged into Gold & Stock. But when the deal was completed Edison felt cheated. All the inventions were his, he claimed. He had done all the work, but he had gotten less than one-third of the money.

Edison was furious. He feared that he had been outsmarted by sly, New York City businessmen. Friends and family had always told him that Eastern businessmen were too clever for an ignorant country boy. While he wasn't stupid, it was true that Edison knew very little about finances. He didn't even know how to cash the $1,500 check he received as his first payment.

In the cool, high-ceilinged bank where Edison went to cash his check, he was confused when the teller pushed the check right back at him. What was going on? Edison could see that the impatient teller was saying something. The man wanted Edison to sign the check on the back. But Edison couldn't hear the teller. He began to think the check was some kind of trick. So he took back the check and stumbled out, eventually returning to the offices of Gold & Stock. They had a good laugh before explaining how to cash a check.

The $1,500 was far less than he wanted, but by taking on William Unger as a partner, Edison was able to use the money to start a new company. Unger was a business associate of Marshall Lefferts, the president of Gold & Stock. As long as Edison was willing to take on Unger as a partner, Lefferts promised to give the new company plenty of orders for stock printers. Edison was ready to try once again to make his fortune. Together, Edison and Unger rented some space in Newark, New Jersey, where they fitted out a workshop and hired about fifty men.

Although Edison & Unger manufactured stock printers, Edison couldn't limit himself to doing that alone. On any day a new idea might catch his fancy, or someone might bring in an invention to ask his opinion. Edison had become famous among other inventors, who came to him for advice. At such times, he might pull all fifty men off their jobs to have them carry out experiments. He would be right there, working alongside them, cheering them on, and occasionally bursting out in a fit of impatience.

Edison was still part of Edison & Unger in October 1870, when he put on a suit and top hat — the business clothes he now used for trips to New York City — and brought a new stock-ticker to Marshall Lefferts at Gold & Stock. Edison's improved ticker solved a problem all other tickers had: They sometimes printed wildly, throwing the whole system out of line.

Lefferts was very interested in what was obviously an important improvement. When he asked the price, Edison hedged. Edison had hoped to sell the patent for $5,000, but he was willing to take as little as $3,000.

"I hadn't the nerve to name such a large sum," Edison explained, "so I said: 'Well, General, suppose you make me an offer.'"

"How would $40,000 strike you?" Lefferts asked.

Forty thousand dollars! As a first-class telegrapher, Edison had earned $1,480 a year. Forty thousand was a fortune.

"This caused me to come as near fainting as I ever got," Edison recalled. "I managed to say I thought it was fair."

Once back in Newark, a gleeful, almost giddy Edison took off his top hat and sailed it across the room, where it landed right in a pan of oil. He was getting ready to do the same with his suit jacket when he was wrestled to the floor by his workers.

Forty thousand dollars! Edison was a rich man, or he would have been, had he been able to hold on to it. Instead he rented a large space in Newark and started another company, the American Telegraph Works. Among his new employees were Charles Batchelor, a mechanic and draftsman, and John Kruesi, a machinist who could put together anything Edison and Batchelor designed. These and many others in that workshop would stay with Edison for all their working lives.

Within weeks, all the money was gone. Edison had spent every cent — and then some — on setting up a shop where he could do all the inventing he wanted. When he was broke again and in terrible debt, he borrowed from some investors who wanted him to invent a high-speed automatic telegraph.

With two laboratories to oversee, Edison was under such pressure that he had little time for the usual human activities, such as sleeping. Besides filling contracts to produce stock-tickers and machinery, he was struggling to come up with new working inventions so that their patents could be sold to get him out of debt.

Edison's first significant invention—an improved stock ticker machine that sold for ten times the amount he had expected. This 1869 effort was the first of thousands of machines and gadgets, from the light bulb to the storage battery that made the automobile possible, that changed the way we live.

To solve the problem of not having enough time to sleep, Edison often decided to dispense with traveling home. Instead, he would lay down on a table and nap in the dusty, noisy workshop. He claimed, though, that he would just as soon do without sleep. "Sleep is an acquired habit," he said once. "Cells don't need sleep. Fish swim about in the water all night. They don't sleep. Even a horse don't sleep. He just stands still and rests. A man don't need any sleep."

When he stayed up all night working, Edison expected his employees to do the same. And they did. John Ott, a draftsman and mechanic who worked for Edison for fifty years, explained why. "Edison made your work interesting," Ott said. "He made me feel that I was making something with him. I wasn't just a workman. And then in those days, we all hoped to get rich with him."

Time wasn't the only thing in short supply. So was money. Edison dealt with both problems in much the same way: He ignored them. Edison was said to keep bills for so long that they turned to dust. When he received large amounts of money, he went out and bought new equipment instead of paying old debts.

Even with his financial problems, Edison, by 1871, was in many ways a successful man. At twenty-four, he was a respected inventor, his work was in demand, and he had two workshops and hundreds of employees. He was also the happiest he had ever been. He loved his work. He even enjoyed a little of the New York City nightlife. Together with Charles Batchelor, who had become a close friend, Edison often steamed across the river to take in a show and eat at the famous Delmonico's restaurant.

Edison's perfect life, however, was interrupted by bad news in April 1871. Edison's mother was ill. While he was thinking about going home for his first visit in more than three years, Nancy Edison died. Edison went back to Michigan for the funeral and quickly returned to bury his grief in work.

In May, when Charles Batchelor married and began spending his free time with his wife rather than with his friend, it became clear that something was missing from Edison's life. He was successful, yes. But he had no real home, and he had no family life. It was around this time that people began to notice that Edison was hovering around a young girl named Mary Stilwell.

6

Settling Down

A T TWENTY-FIVE, Thomas Edison was handsome enough to turn the heads of the young women who worked at the Gold & Stock Telegraph Company. He had thick black hair, bright blue eyes, and a jaunty mustache. Although he still spoke with a country twang, he no longer brought the country habit of chewing tobacco into downtown New York. With a fat cigar, a well-made suit, and a silk top hat, he was the picture of success and self-confidence.

But there was another reason why Edison turned heads at Gold & Stock. It was his strange behavior. Ever since the summer of 1871, when Mary Stilwell took a seat in one of the company's wooden work stations, Edison had been spending an unusual amount of time there. He was trying to get up the nerve to say something to the shy, pretty young girl with the slim figure and thick blond ringlets. While Mary struggled to ignore Tom, her fingers shaking as she typed Morse signals onto telegraph tape, Tom just stood there, speechless.

As Edison inched silently nearer, day by day, the

other typists watched with fascination. Edison noticed the heads turning and the tittering, but he paid them no attention. He'd show them. He wasn't tongue-tied. He was going to say something — right now! But what?

When it came to talking to men, Edison had no problem. Even though casual talk was sometimes hard because of his deafness, men liked and respected him. Besides having an impressive mind, Edison had a good collection of funny stories. With women, on the other hand, he had no idea how to begin. Each day he pressed a little closer, but still said nothing. When Tom was finally standing so close he was practically breathing down her neck, Mary dropped her hands in her lap. She couldn't go on.

Like Thomas Edison, Mary Stilwell came from a family with a well-educated mother and a father who never made enough money to keep his family comfortable. But even though Mary was working to help the family pay their bills, she had the reserved manners of the upper classes. Those manners were little help as she sat hunched over her keys, weighed down by the presence of Thomas Edison behind her.

"Oh, Mr. Edison," Mary said, nervous and embarrassed. "I can always tell when you are near me!"

A few days later, still struggling to find the perfect words, Tom said abruptly, "What do you think of me, little girl? Do you like me?"

Mary didn't know what to say. The truth was, he frightened her.

"Don't be in a hurry about telling me," Edison continued, afraid she would reject him. "It doesn't matter much," he added, "unless you would like to marry me."

In her surprise, Mary Stilwell let out a nervous gasp.

"Oh, I mean it," he assured her, all the while fearing that she thought he was the most awful dunce. "Think it over, talk to your mother about it and let me know as soon as convenient. Tuesday, say." As soon as those words were out, he wondered how he could be so stupid. Tuesday was not nearly enough time. "Next week, Tuesday, I mean." With that he backed up a few steps before turning and making a quick exit.

Mary must have found him an acceptable suitor. The next Sunday they met outside the Newark Sunday school where Mary taught, and Tom took her, along with her sister Alice, for a carriage ride. After that, they began to meet after work for dinner and a show. By November 1871, Mary agreed to marry Tom. She had been quite overwhelmed by him. He was so much older than she, twenty-five to her sixteen. He knew so much more about the world, and he was so important and seemed so rich.

The ceremony was held on December 25, Christmas Day 1871. But the couple had barely set foot in their newly rented home before Mary got her first taste of what marriage to Thomas Edison would be like. Work always came first with him, and its demands were endless. Instead of flooding his bride with attention, he immediately began to think about a stock-ticker that had been causing him problems. Tom described the ticker to Mary, trying to draw her into that part of his life, but he was disappointed to learn that she had no idea what he was talking about and cared little. Within an hour he asked if she minded if he went down to the shop for a little while. The ticker was preying on his mind. He thought he had an idea that might correct it.

Mary was too cowed by him to refuse. So Tom left her

all alone, still in her wedding clothes. Once he got to the shop, everything but the ticker completely left his mind. He forgot about eating. He forgot about his young bride. He completely forgot about the time. Edison kept working until someone barged into his office and asked him what he was doing there at midnight on his wedding day. Midnight? At first, Edison let only part of his mind leave the work on his desk. Then he shifted gears. Midnight! "I must go home," he said, jumping up and grabbing his hat. "I was just married today."

Edison soon settled down into a married life — of sorts. He still worked into the small hours of the morning, and often went over to New York with his friend Charles Batchelor or others for a night on the town. The difference was that now, when he went home to throw himself fully clothed into bed, he went to a home and a wife rather than to a rooming house and landlady.

Edison's finances, on the other hand, were more unsettled than ever. In October 1871, Edison's investors had taken over American Telegraph Works, where he did most of his inventing. In June 1872, William Unger told Edison that he couldn't stand Edison's undisciplined business ways. Unger wanted to end their partnership, sell the shop, and split the profits. That would have left Edison with nowhere to work, something he couldn't let happen. Instead he decided to buy out Unger. Edison took out a loan for $10,000 that he had to pay back in two years, with interest. He was now loaded down with debt.

At home, Mary was handling money in much the same manner Tom did at work. She bought all her household needs on credit and left the butcher and the baker waiting. The large allowance Tom gave her was spent on candy, clothes, and trips to the city.

Under financial pressure at work and home, Tom put in long hours. Even though he sometimes worked so hard that he fell ill and went home to collapse, Edison was optimistic. All he needed, he kept saying, was one good invention. Then his money troubles would be over.

For the rest of 1872 and most of 1873, Edison thought his most promising work was the automatic telegraph, which sent messages at high speed. Unfortunately, he couldn't find a buyer. Western Union didn't think it would work. The Atlantic & Pacific Telegraph Company, a new company competing with Western Union, didn't think an automatic telegraph would help them reach their goal. That goal was to take over Western Union.

When it looked as if the automatic telegraph was going nowhere, Edison pressed forward on another invention that he had in the works: the quadruplex. Western Union already had a duplex, which Joseph Stearns had developed before Edison could get one to work properly. The Stearns duplex could send two messages over one wire, but only in opposite directions. That turned out to be far less useful than expected. Telegraph traffic was much like commuter traffic. There was always a crush in one direction or the other. Edison's quadruplex, which could send two messages each way, relieved that problem. Western Union was interested, and so was Atlantic & Pacific.

Pressed by a July deadline on his $10,000 debt, and by an unhappy wife, Edison began testing his quadruplex in February 1874. By the end of June, he was ready to show it to William Orton, the president of Western Union. But while Edison was trying to set up a demonstration date, Orton went on vacation. He left town and wasn't due back until July 7. That was seven days too late. Edison's $10,000 loan was due on July 1. The bank was threatening to foreclose on the Newark shop. Edison managed to hold off the bank by paying the sheriff $5 a day, but he was in a frenzy and his stomach was in knots. He was chewing tobacco non-stop, which made matters even worse. On July 7, Orton took one look at Edison, who was running his hands through his unkempt hair, and knew immediately that the man was desperate.

Orton wanted Edison's quadruplex, but he wanted to get it at the lowest possible price. When a man has creditors hounding him as Edison did, he is in no position to enter into lengthy negotiations. Time was on Orton's side, and he made the most of it. Orton told Edison that Western Union wanted to buy the quadruplex, but he made an offer that was too low for Edison to accept. The two men negotiated for several months, but Orton's offers were always too low. Finally, in December 1874, they reached an agreement. Edison didn't like it much, but he had no real choice. But before Edison had gotten a cent, Orton again left town.

While Orton was gone, Jay Gould, head of the Atlantic & Pacific, came to see Edison's quadruplex. The next day, he offered Edison $30,000 in cash and $75,000 in stock to be paid later. Edison took it. When Western Union heard about the sale of the quadruplex, they sued, claiming that they already had a contract with Edison. Jay Gould used Western Union's claim as an excuse to hold onto Edison's $75,000 worth of stock.

Years of lawsuits followed. In the end, Jay Gould got the quadruplex, took over Western Union, and never gave Edison one share of the promised $75,000 worth of stock. In the meantime, the $30,000 Edison got in December 1874 made it possible for him to pay his most pressing debts, give some money to Mary, and even buy a business for his brother Pitt, back in Michigan.

All in all, Edison had managed to become quite well off. Besides owning the Newark shop and part of a business in Michigan, he had also invented the mimeograph machine, which he had sold for part interest in a mimeograph business. The mimeograph is a very successful duplicator that is still used in schools all over the United States. By the spring of 1875, though, creditors were again after Edison. He was property rich and cash poor. Mary, too, was pressing him. Pregnant with their second child, she was tired of living, with her baby daughter, in the small apartment over a Newark drugstore to which the family had moved. She wanted desperately to own her own home.

The answer to his problems seemed clear. On December 29, 1875, just twelve days before Mary gave birth to their second child, Thomas Alva Edison, Jr., Edison bought a house and some property in the quiet farming village of Menlo Park, New Jersey. There he would surely be able to produce more and spend less.

7

Menlo Park

BACK IN THE days before television, news was the best entertainment going in a small town like Menlo Park, New Jersey. And the most riveting news is local news. That's why, when the Menlo Park farmers gathered in the general store after a day of straining behind their plow horses to furrow and plant, many of them were talking about that Edison fellow. He was having a foundation dug over by the railroad tracks on a corner of old Carman's farm. Rumors flew about the thirty-by-hundred-foot foundation and the two-story, wood-frame building that went up above it. It didn't look like a home, and there were too many windows for a barn. Some people thought it would be a meetinghouse. In fact, it was a laboratory, and Edison had ambitious plans for it. He was going to turn out "a minor invention every ten days and a big thing every six months or so."

Most of the people of Menlo Park never really understood what Edison had planted in their midst in the summer of 1876. Years later, long after Edison had left, two local farmers were seen walking around the Edison property. As they kicked a stone in the overgrown yard and paused to look inside a crumbling building, they said what a shame that a once well-kept farm had been allowed to go to ruin. A lab worker by the name of David Marshall, who was in Menlo Park on a visit, overheard the two old-timers. "I don't suppose," wrote Marshall in his book, *Recollections of Edison,* "that either of those farmers realized that a crop had been harvested on that old farm that was worth more to the world than a thousand years of the crops that had been harvested before." Menlo Park had played host to the world's first commercial laboratory — a lab devoted to inventing useful things.

By the summer of 1878, Menlo Park had already been the source of numerous minor inventions, some as silly as a refillable cigar, a perfumed imitation rose, and a musical telephone. Others were more practical, such as the electric sewing machine, electric shears, and electric dentist's drill. Edison also invented a telegraph and telephone that printed messages.

By early 1879, his phonograph was delighting and amazing people across the country. After producing hundreds of record players, he sent them to the towns and cities of America, where crowds of people paid an admission price to hear "Yankee Doodle." It was perhaps his most popular invention. But it was only the beginning.

Tom and his nephew, Charley Edison, his brother Pitt's son, experimented in Menlo Park with an "etheric force" that Tom had discovered earlier. They sent this force, which turned out to be radio waves, from the laboratory to Edison's house nearby and then many miles beyond. After playing around with it and taking out a few patents on it, they eventually lost interest. Decades later, when Guglielmo Marconi tried to patent his radio in the United States, he found, to his chagrin, that Edison had already laid claim to some of Marconi's discoveries.

Edison's major inventions before 1878 — the quadruplex, the microphone, an improved telephone, and the phonograph — were such astonishing advances that people of the time began to believe that Edison could do anything. As a joke, one newspaper ran a story saying that Edison had figured out how to make food out of dirt, and many people believed it. Though he had become known as the Wizard of Menlo Park, he had yet to do his most impressive work.

Anyone who caught a glimpse of Edison while he was living and working at Menlo Park during this time would never have thought he was a man of much importance. When Tom ambled out of his house during the summer of 1878, he looked more like a mechanic than a great inventor. Instead of a suit, he wore smelly, rumpled work clothes spotted with chemical stains. If his hands weren't buried in his pants pockets, he was probably running one through his graying hair. He was only thirty-one years old, but he looked older as he walked, head down, through the gate in the picket fence and on toward the main building.

To get to his laboratory inside the building, Edison had to walk past his office, with its inevitable pile of dusty bills, and past the cramped library just opposite. Since much of Edison's work at that time had to do with the properties of carbon, the library was piled high with every journal and every book that had anything of in-

Edison, age 30, in 1877 with his favorite invention, the original tinfoil phonograph. Edison exhibited the phonograph at the National Academy of Science in Washington and demonstrated it for President Ulysses S. Grant at the White House.

terest to say about the element. Edison had read it all. Whenever he had anything to learn, he still studied up on it the way he had during his telegrapher days.

The first thing Edison did every morning was shuffle through the lab. When there was a major project going on, several assistants would be assigned to it, all working on different parts. Edison checked in with each worker to see how the work in progress was faring. He asked questions, and the lab workers shouted back their answers. The only one who knew how each experiment fit into the larger puzzle was the "old man," as his staff called him — Edison himself.

While giving orders for further research on various inventions, Edison was often joined by his daughter, Marion, a spunky, blond, five-year-old nicknamed "Dot," after the Morse code. Tom Jr., two years old, had been given the nickname of "Dash." For the most part, however, Thomas Edison was far from attentive as a father. Dot, with her independence and energy, had wormed her way into his heart. Sometimes Edison picked her up and bounced her on his knee. But after a few minutes he would get caught up in a problem and forget about her. Dot would then slip down to the floor and play with models of her father's inventions, ignoring the cigar smoke and the rancid chemical smells around her.

In August 1878, however, Edison didn't have a major project to absorb all his time, so he often went fishing or took his little daughter by the hand and walked her home. The Edisons owned a farmhouse a couple of minutes' walk from the lab. Inside the five-bedroom house, one of Mary's three servants would meet Edison at the door and take Dot off to get washed up. Edison then walked into the dining room, turning away from the parlor with its piano, mirrors, and heavily cushioned seats. It was a parlor the likes of which no one else in Menlo Park had. No one could afford such furniture, not to mention the lace curtains and Oriental rugs.

In the late afternoon, Edison often came home for a bite to eat and a nap. As Edison sat down, Mary sometimes joined him, her fine clothes rustling as she moved. Mary was expecting their third child, and she was miserable. She was having a difficult pregnancy, and even though she was considered a grand lady in Menlo Park, Mary was lonely and nervous. Her husband talked to anyone who showed up at his lab, but he hardly ever talked to her. Neither did the people of Menlo Park, who were awed by her city ways, fine clothes, and expensive tastes. Edison fit right in at the general store, exchanging stories with the rest of the menfolk. But Mary had no friends. In her misery, she was eating a pound of chocolate every day, and she gained an immense amount of weight.

As each day wore into night, Thomas Edison usually gained energy and really came to life. On August 28, 1878, however, Edison had little to do. For once, Mary was able to get a little attention in the late afternoon. Her husband agreed to take her and the children for a buggy ride. When he got home, he still didn't rush off to work. There was a reporter from the *New York Sun* waiting to see him, and Edison took him for a tour.

As Edison told the *Sun* reporter, he was "off his center" at the moment. He wasn't doing much, and the laboratory reflected that listlessness. The evening sun, slanting in through jars of chemicals lined up near the windows, "cast a lurid green light upon the floor," the reporter wrote. Half-finished machinery was lying around the laboratory tables gathering dust. So were a half dozen new, improved phonographs. In the back of the room, the reporter found a pipe organ and went over to play a few notes. When Edison and his men were working through the night, they usually took a dinner break at midnight and gathered around that organ for some music and singing. Now the organ was out of tune; it hadn't been used for a while.

There was some work going on. Several kerosene lamps were "sputtering and smoking while a boy scraped carbon from their chimneys," as the *Sun* account read. This carbon would be pressed into buttons and used to make carbon transmitters for telephones. In the middle of one table was a machine Edison called an "aerophone." He said he was going to use it to talk to a friend in Ohio. He also showed the *Sun* reporter some ink that, when dry, left raised marks that the blind might be able to read. This was one of his many ideas that he never developed. Louis Braille's system of raised dots was much easier to distinguish by touch.

Nothing in the *New York Sun*'s article gave any hint that within weeks Edison would make an announcement that would cause turmoil in the stock market. Nevertheless, on October 11, 1878, gas stocks plummeted. Word had leaked out that the Wizard of Menlo Park had formed an electric company. Edison was going into the business of supplying electric light. Soon, he said, he would light up the towns and cities of America!

Many inventors had tried, but no one had been able to make an incandescent light bulb, an electric light, that did not quickly flash out. Something called an arc light was beginning to be used in the streets of New York City. Arc lights, which were hooked up to enormous generators called dynamos, were big, bulky, and very bright. The light was formed when electrical currents jumped across a gap between two carbon rods, or electrodes, and made a continuous spark. But arc lamps required an enormous amount of current and lasted only a few hours. No one had been able to figure out how to produce a light bulb that would use less current, stay lighted without burning up its electrode, and be soft enough for lighting a home. In addition, there was no such thing as an electric plug or socket, and no electric meters or insulated wires. There were electric generators, a central source for producing electricity, but none that could power up even as small a town as Menlo Park. All these things were necessary in order to make electric light practical, but none of them existed.

Yet on October 20, 1878, Thomas Alva Edison claimed that he would wire up Menlo Park and give a "grand exhibition" of his new electric light, and he would do it in just six weeks.

8

The Dark Before the Dawn

RAINDROPS FELL THICK on the puddles of Menlo Park. Despite the weather, a bootless, hatless Thomas Edison slogged through the mud on the evening of October 20, 1878. A reporter from the *New York Sun* was at his side while his five-year-old daughter, Dot, darted behind them. Every few seconds she stopped to play in a puddle and then raced to catch up.

It was a quiet Sunday evening at the Edison plant. The place was nearly empty. After hanging their dripping jackets on a coatrack in the corner of his cluttered office, Edison leaned over his desk to turn up the gas lamp.

"When I remember how the gas companies used to treat me," Edison said, settling back into his chair and lighting a cigar, "I must say that it gives me great pleasure to get square with them."

The gas company, one of Edison's many creditors back in Newark, had been particularly impatient with his casual attitude about paying bills. They wanted

71

their money, and to get it, they had threatened to cut off his supply of gas.

Now Edison had gotten even. In the middle of September 1878, Edison started telling newspaper reporters that he was on the verge of coming out with a practical electric light. Actually, he was far from it, but he believed he knew where all previous inventors working on electric lights had gone wrong. After staying up for several days and nights working on the problem, and after making a few patent proposals, Edison made his announcement. He knew he was painting himself into a corner, but he didn't care. He was sure he had solved the central problem; all he had to do was overcome a few related problems. Besides, he needed publicity to drum up some investors.

It worked. By October 2, an agreement to form an electric light company was ironed out. Edison would own half the company and receive financing from the other partners to pay for his experiments. The first installment, $50,000, arrived on October 15. By then, news of the Edison Electric Light Company had leaked out, and gas-stock owners, both in New York and London, went on a selling spree. The value of their stock plummeted.

"Are you positive that you have found a light that will take the place of gas and be much cheaper to consumers?" the reporter asked.

Edison, thirty-one years old, cupped his hand behind his ear. The reporter had to repeat his question.

"Have you found a light that will take the place of gas?" the reported yelled.

"There can be no doubt about it," Edison answered.

"Is it an electric light?" the writer yelled.

"It is," Edison said. "Electricity, and nothing else."

With a calmness and cheerfulness that made it seem like everything was perfectly under control, Edison led the journalist up the wooden stairway to his workroom. The lab was empty and only dimly lit. In the near darkness, the many wires that hung down looked like tentacles dropping from an ivy plant gone berserk. The flickering gaslight made the shadows sway and jerk. If Edison had let out a piercing, mad-scientist laugh, it would not have been out of place. He brought the reporter over to a table in the back of the room, joking and talking all the while.

A round lamp socket was bolted to this table; wires from its base led to a battery. Edison slipped a bulb in the socket. It would be many months before one of Edison's laboratory assistants would come up with the idea of putting grooves in the bulb and socket so that they screwed firmly together. In the meantime, the least jiggle could send a bulb crashing.

"You turn the cock," Edison said as he demonstrated. "The electric connection is made, the platinum burner catches a proper degree of heat, and there is your light." Inside the thick, hand-blown glass bulb, the filament, a spiral of platinum wire, seemed to grow as it changed from red to yellow and then to white.

After getting a good-sized dose of his visitor's admiration, Edison turned the switch in the opposite direction. He had to, for in another couple of minutes the platinum filament would have overheated and flashed out. Edison had not yet figured out how to make a filament, the burner inside a bulb, that would produce a steady light without burning up. Nevertheless, he went on to tell the *Sun* reporter that after two days and two nights of nonstop work, he had discovered "the necessary secret" of the incandescent bulb. With a twinkle in his eye, Edison went on to say that the solution had come to him suddenly, "the same as in the secret of the speaking phonograph."

But there was nothing accidental or, despite what people said, wizardlike about the way Edison worked. "Genius," he often said, "is one percent inspiration and ninety-nine percent perspiration." He worked methodically, testing one possibility after another. He figured out what would work only after seeing what had failed.

"In trying to perfect a thing," Edison later wrote in his diary, "I sometimes run straight up against a granite wall one-hundred feet high. If, after trying and trying and trying again, I can't get over it, I turn to something else. Then, someday, it may be months or it may be years later, something is discovered . . . which I recognize may help me to scale the last part of that wall."

Still, if this were all there was to it, anyone in Edison's laboratory could have done what Edison did. They all worked hard. But they lacked that other one percent of Edison's invention equation: inspiration. It was Edison alone who could take that brilliant leap necessary to come up with a creative solution to a difficult problem.

The subdivision of electric current was that "necessary secret" he mentioned during his interview on that Sunday night in October 1878. The arc lights that were in use at the time required so much current that they were not practical. Before Edison, no one knew how to take the electricity that came from a battery or from one of the crude generators and make small amounts available for small jobs without so much waste that it became too expensive. This problem was the biggest stumbling block to the invention of the practical electric light.

A British scientist named John Tyndall had also been trying to subdivide electric current in 1878. Tyndall came to the problem with the same information as Edison. He experimented along the same lines as Edison. If he had taken one last, small step, he, and not Edison, might have invented an incandescent light bulb that lasted.

"The next step was so obvious," Tyndall was told during a court battle over one of Edison's patents. "Why did you not take it?"

"Because," Tyndall answered, "I was not Thomas A. Edison."

The answer that Tyndall never found was a filament with high electrical resistance. Low-resistance filaments require too much power to be efficient sources of light. In addition, without high resistance, electricity merely dribbled through the circuit. The use of high-resistance filaments permits a small amount of current under greater electric pressure, or voltage, to produce all the light anyone would want.

Electricity flowing through a wire acts something like water in a pipe. A small amount of water moving through a large pipe will drip rather than flow steadily. There will be little pressure. But pump that same amount of water through a straw, which resists the flow by restricting it, and there's plenty of pressure. Without resistance, so much power is needed to build up electric pressure and keep a light burning steadily that electric light would never have been cheap enough to compete with gas.

Of course, in 1878 there were no electric mains, or lines, to carry any power. The high-resistance bulb, which was proving difficult to develop, was itself just one small part of the enormous system that Edison had in mind. Wiring, meters, and insulators were needed. He had to have central boxes and fuses, to say nothing of outlets and sockets, plugs and more.

And what about power? He couldn't use batteries to light a city. The generators that existed were crude versions of what he needed. His generator needed to produce much more electricity — without exploding, without shaking nearby buildings, and without creating unbearable amounts of noise and smoke.

The circuitry and the generator and the hardware needed for an electric system occupied corners of Edison's mind. All of them were necessary if he was ever going to make any money out of the electric light. But it was all worthless without the bulb, and the bulb was a tougher problem than he had originally thought. All his filaments fizzled.

The rain was still beating on the windows when Edison put down his cigar and took out some chewing tobacco. After politely offering it to his interviewer from the *Sun*, Edison bit off a chunk for himself. He knew he was facing a smooth granite wall with this electric bulb, but he didn't want anyone else to know that. So he looked straight into that reporter's eyes and proceeded to lie through his teeth.

"The only thing to be accurately determined is its economy," Edison said. "I am already positive it will be cheaper than gas, but have not yet determined how much cheaper." He had a few bugs to work out, he said, but he expected the light to be "in practical operation" in six weeks.

The six weeks came and went, and still Edison and his assistants struggled. During those last months of 1878, Edison's factory had focused on two projects. One was the telephone, his only money-maker at the time. The other was that frustrating electric light.

The lab was filled with men hunched over the tables in the large upstairs room. Charles Batchelor, Edison's closest friend, had moved to Menlo Park. With Batchelor working by his side, Edison was at his most productive. Batchelor knew how to focus Edison's mind and turn his ideas into concrete plans. To keep Batchelor happy, Edison had made him a partner, paying him a salary and a part of the profits. Batchelor was working on both the telephone and the electric light.

Jim Adams was working on the telephone, but he was off in Europe, serving as Edison's telephone expert overseas. Tom's nephew, Charley Edison, was supervising the telephone work in Menlo Park. Eighteen-year-old Charley was being groomed to take over the business someday, but his uncle's retirement was not expected anytime soon. Edison was only thirty-two years old.

Most of the other lab workers spent their time making filaments from all kinds of metals, hooking them up to batteries, and staring at them as they lit up and then burned out. They tried carbon, iron, copper, steel, titanium, cobalt, and zinc. They used alloys and compounds of these and other elements. One after another, the filaments were twisted or cut into different shapes, lengths, and thicknesses. Slowly and carefully, each handmade filament was sealed into a glass bulb and air was pumped out to create a vacuum. If the filament didn't break and the glass didn't burst while the pump was going, the finished bulb would be placed in a socket.

Each time a test began, Edison and his assistants held their breath. Maybe this bulb, this time, had the filament with the right properties. As the filament lit up, its staying power was clocked: one minute . . . two minutes . . . three minutes . . . four. Could this be the one? Every time, in hundreds of trials, the filament melted, shot out sparks, or simply burned itself up.

"I never allow myself to become discouraged," Edison wrote in his diary. He considered each experiment a success. "We learned for a certainty that the thing couldn't be done that way," he told his assistants, "and that we would have to try some other way."

On December 2, 1878, a reporter from the *New York Herald* came to see how Edison was doing. Other scientists, he told Edison, had begun to doubt that Edison had invented an incandescent bulb.

"So I see," Edison said, leaning back in his chair and smiling broadly, as if everything his critics said was a bunch of hogwash. Those scientists, he went on to say, were unaware of a law of electricity that he had discovered. "If certain conditions are brought about," Edison said, electric power can be used. "These conditions are exceedingly difficult to obtain."

"Have you obtained them?" the reporter asked.

"I have," Edison lied.

The search continued. On January 29, 1879, Edison twisted nickel into a spiral, attached it to platinum wires, and hooked it up to a battery. As he watched, the nickel flashed so brightly that he was temporarily blinded. Even before his sight had returned to normal, he gave another interview. His system would be working within a year, he claimed, trying to appear as if everything was going as expected.

By now, Edison had made a lot of promises, and people were starting to lose faith. "As day after day, week after week, and month after month passes," wrote the New York *Daily Graphic,* "doubts as to the practicability and value of his . . . inventions begin to be entertained in the public mind." *Puck,* a humor magazine, wrote that Edison "can do a great deal and he thinks he can do everything."

The criticism may have hurt Edison's pride, but there were far worse problems ahead. His investors were getting nervous, with some threatening to unload their stock just when Edison was about to ask for more money. Edison realized he had to do something to reassure them. The best way to do that would be to show them how well things were going — if only they were. He still hadn't found a high-resistance filament. He had to make do with what he had. A demonstration was set for March 22, 1879.

"We was all night bringing up twelve lamps in a vacuum," Edison wrote in his journal of March 16, 1879. "Worked all day Sunday, all night Sunday night, all day Monday."

Edison wasn't much of a believer in the need for sleep, but he did understand that men needed to eat. No matter how much pressure they were under, everyone stopped work at midnight for their dinner break. Usually a young boy was sent to a nearby farmer's wife to bring back a steaming cauldron of soup or stew. For a little while, everyone relaxed. After dinner they gathered around the pipe organ and someone would play. One of the mechanics played the violin fairly well. So most nights, before they resumed work, the muffled sounds of music and song rang out in the otherwise sleeping countryside.

The investors arrived on the appointed evening, a Saturday. Edison himself met them at the railroad station and walked them over to the lab. He was his most charming, telling stories, joking, and keeping the talk and laughter going. At the same time, he wasn't at all certain that the demonstration he had planned would do the trick. He was taking a big risk.

Everyone was in a good mood as they gathered in the machine shop. Sixteen bulbs were set in sockets above the work benches, and there was plenty of time to get a good look at the glass bulbs that would, Edison assured his visitors, revolutionize the world. They would change the way people worked and lived, he went on; they would turn the night into day.

When he was ready, Edison turned to his head mechanic, John Kruesi, and gave him the nod. The gas lamps were turned off one by one. As the room dimmed, the anticipation grew.

"Turn on the juice, slowly," Edison instructed Kruesi. Gradually, the sixteen lamps glowed red, then orange.

"A little more, please," Edison said. The lamps went from orange to yellow.

If Edison had not been nearly deaf, he would have heard the investors gasp as the electric lights turned a beautiful, soft white. They were awed. They were amazed. They were delighted. Then one lamp started to flicker. Across the room, sparks flew from another. Suddenly a light near a group of men flared so brightly that they turned away from it, shielding their eyes and jumping when it burst. Edison and Batchelor began to put resistors in the lamps, in a frantic effort to get control of the system. But it was no use. A few seconds later, glass was shattering all over the room.

9

"My Light Is Perfected"

"I NEVER REALLY become interested in something until it seems hopeless," Edison once said. When the last bulb blew during his demonstration in March 1879, things must have appeared fairly hopeless indeed. After six months and $50,000, Edison had learned a lot, but mostly he had discovered what wouldn't work.

As the investors filed somberly out of Edison's machine shop and gathered in the library to wait for the next train, Edison made two quick decisions. First, he wisely chose not to point out that their investment money had paid for the expensive furniture and plush new library they were using. Second, he decided to convince them that the electric bulb was coming along just fine. It was true, he had to admit, that exploding bulbs were of limited commercial value. But the bulbs would have worked, Edison insisted, if his generator had run at an even level. The generator was the problem, Edison said, and that was a minor bug. The generator would be easy to correct.

If the investors were convinced, they didn't show it. A few days later, the stock-market value of Edison Electric Light fell. At the same time, gas stocks began to rise. Unlike Edison, the investors didn't view failure as a discovery of what wouldn't work, a necessary and inevitable step in the process of invention. To them it was just failure, plain and simple.

Despite what Edison said about the generator, his biggest problem was actually the incandescent bulb. He had used platinum filaments for the demonstration because platinum produced a bright, comfortable light. But platinum had a lot of drawbacks. For one thing, it melted too easily. To keep the wire from melting and blowing out, Edison put a regulator inside each bulb to reduce the current when the filament got too hot. These regulators never worked perfectly, but even if they had, there was another problem. Platinum was very expensive. The price of each bulb, with its filament and regulator, was about $98. That was equal to about ten weeks' wages for most people. Most important, platinum's electrical resistance was too low. The biggest stumbling block to a practical electric light still remained: Edison had not yet found a filament with high electrical resistance.

Now that no new money was forthcoming from his stockholders, Edison found himself in a familiar bind: debt. He had hundreds of IOU's floating around Menlo Park, and he had to start making good on them. To do that, he shifted gears in the lab. He took nearly everyone off the light project, which was going nowhere fast, and put them to work on the telephone.

Orders for telephones had been bringing in a small amount of money for months, but in the spring of 1879,

Edison had a chance to win a big contract. He had a demonstration scheduled for May before the British Royal Society in London, England. Europeans were as interested as Americans in Edison's inventions. He had already patented inventions in Europe, and he had even set up companies overseas. If the British liked Edison's equipment, they would give him a large order and his financial problems would be solved.

Jim Adams was in London as Edison's telephone expert, but Edison also sent over his nephew Charley. That proved to be a mistake. Edison's stomach turned sour as telegrams flew back and forth. Things weren't going well. Charley was taking over the project, and Adams was angry. In his fury, Adams abandoned the telephone demonstration and went over to Paris to work for a different Edison company, Edison European Telephone. Then, on Sunday, May 4, 1879, another telegram arrived with the news that Adams had died, at thirty-five, from a combination of alcoholism and tuberculosis.

Jim Adams had been at Edison's side through some of Edison's toughest years. He had helped with some of Edison's most difficult problems. When news of his death reached Menlo Park, Edison was stunned. Between this and the disastrous light demonstration, Edison felt like everything was falling apart.

After a death, many people turn to religion or family for comfort. However, Edison was never much of a churchgoer; neither would he turn to his family. When Adams died, Edison's family wasn't even around. He had sent them to Florida in February to take advantage of the mild weather, because Tom Jr. was sick and Mary had never fully recovered from her difficult third pregnancy. When Adams died, he turned for comfort to what he loved most — his work.

Fortunately, work soon provided a big boost. The telephone demonstration was held on May 10, 1879, and it was a great success. London decided to buy Edison's system. About a week later, Edison had a $25,000 advance to pay for British telephones. Now that he had some cash, he could go on working on the light.

Back in Menlo Park, the mood began to pick up. The parts to the puzzle of the electric light were gradually coming together. Upstairs, at one end of the lab, Edison had a new vacuum pump. He knew that filaments burned up in the air's oxygen, but he had never been able to get a perfect vacuum. This noisy new pump was the best available, and he had worked on it to make it better. Downstairs in the machine shop, Edison had his men working on a new generator. Even if he never came up with an electric bulb, he would at least be able to make some money from the improved generator.

No matter what he was doing, Edison never lost track of any experiment that was going on in the lab. He was always right there for his men, urging them on when they were tired, joking with them when they felt discouraged or disappointed, leading them forward with his excitement and enthusiasm.

Thomas Edison spent two weeks of that long, hot summer at a table beside Batchelor, collecting soot. With shirts off and perspiration dripping over their eyebrows, the two men spent hour after hour scraping soot off the glass of smoking kerosene lamps and shaping it into telephone transmitter buttons to be sent off to

London. Carbon was a good substance to use because it was cheap and had a high melting point.

Through July and August, Edison also experimented with new regulators and coated the platinum filaments with different insulating materials. He was trying to protect the glass from the heat of the filament. Without air as a buffer, the glass kept cracking.

On Friday, September 26, 1879, Edison made a filament of a platinum alloy, insulated it with magnesium oxide, attached it to a regulator, and had it sealed inside a bulb. After the air was pumped out, the bulb was put in a socket and turned on. As soon as it lit, everyone could see that this bulb was not the final answer. Its electric resistance, which is measured in ohms, was three — not nearly enough. The bulb didn't glow very brightly, either. But it did do one thing that other bulbs had failed to do: It kept on burning.

For hour after hour, the dimly lit bulb sat in its socket while two or more men stared at it and talked quietly. One by one, the rest of the men who worked at Menlo Park stopped by to get a look at the bulb that didn't go out. It stayed lit for 13 hours and 38 minutes, proving that it was possible to keep a filament lit in a vacuum.

Several days later, Batchelor noticed that the carbon transmitters they were making for the telephone were perfectly insulated. He thought it was because of the silicon on which the transmitter rested. So he suggested that Edison try using silicon as an insulator. The discussion gave Edison a different idea. Why not try carbon itself as filament? Carbon has an extremely high melting point, and it was cheap. Edison had tried carbon filaments before, but that was months ago, before he had perfected the vacuum pump. Now his mind

The inventor in his laboratory. Edison's expertise came in great part from his experimentation with chemicals and electrical currents. Note his hands and fingernails, stained and discolored from the materials and substances with which he worked.

started racing. What would happen if he put a carbon filament in a perfect vacuum?

On Monday, October 13, 1879, Edison tested a piece of carbon. It glowed in the center and emitted light from both ends. However, as the carbon heated up, its electrical resistance went down. For the next forty hours, Edison and his assistants worked nearly nonstop, combining different materials with carbon to raise its electrical resistance. Edison took off only three hours for sleep, and even then he never left the lab. He just curled up under a table for a quick rest. Everyone worked furiously until, on Tuesday night, the vacuum pump broke. It was four days before a new one could be delivered. Edison was infuriated.

On Friday night, October 17, Edison was returning to his experiments with carbon when a telegram arrived from Europe. Charley Edison had fallen seriously ill. All work stopped while Edison's closest friends stayed with him, waiting. On Sunday the dreaded news came. Charley, just nineteen years old, was dead. Edison was devastated. But he knew only one way to make himself feel better — concentrate on work.

On that very same Sunday night, Edison connected a carbon rod that glowed more brightly than any platinum filament ever had. Finally he had a filament that was an improvement on platinum. Carbon gave off better light, it didn't need any regulators to keep it from getting too hot, and it was cheap. Its one drawback was its low electric resistance. The carbon rod measured only two ohms.

Pushing his personal tragedy out of his mind, Edison focused on how to raise carbon's electrical resistance. Sitting in a corner with his feet up on a table and his chin slumped down on his chest, he looked asleep, but he was thinking. Perhaps, he thought, the solution was to make the carbon filament thinner and longer. If the same amount of current ran through a thinner filament, the resistance should go up, just like water pressure when water flows through a straw instead of a pipe.

For two days, Edison had Batchelor struggling to make carbon wires by pushing lampblack through a mold, like pasta through a pasta machine. The plan was to attach the thin carbon wire to the wires of a bulb. But every time Batchelor tried, he failed. The carbon kept crumbling. Finally, on Tuesday, October 21, Edison suggested they use sewing thread — which was already the right shape — and bake it in an oven to turn it to carbon.

All night, Edison and Batchelor worked with the carbonized threads. One at a time, the baked threads were lifted gently from the oven and brought to the connecting wires of a bulb. But one after another, the carbon threads broke. They were either too delicate to take from the oven, or they cracked as they were being attached.

After hours of agonizing work, a carbon thread was successfully screwed onto the wires. But the thread broke as the glassblower sealed it inside the bulb. After several more tries, Batchelor finally got a carbon thread sealed in a bulb — only to see everyone's hopes dashed when the bulb was dropped on the way from the glassblower's shed to the upstairs lab. Daylight was breaking, and they had to start all over again.

It was nine o'clock in the morning on Wednesday, October 22, 1879, before a bulb was finally ready. It was placed, oh so carefully, in a socket, and the current was turned on. For a few seconds, a very, very dim light was seen, and then the filament quickly flashed out. Another failure? Not at all. The resistance on this carbon thread had measured 113 ohms. Edison had finally found his high-resistance filament. With it Edison had overcome the last problem. Under various conditions, carbon filaments had given off a strong light, lasted a long time, and had high electrical resistance. Edison knew it was just a matter of time before he put it all together.

For the next few weeks, Edison was dancing around the laboratory in his joy and excitement. He barely ate. He never went home to change or sleep. He just kept trying all kinds of carbon filaments: wood shavings, fish line, coconut shell, twine, and even a red hair from a man's beard. But it was a horseshoe-shaped piece of cardboard, boiled in sugar and alcohol and then baked in an oven, that gave the best results. With his cardboard filament Edison produced a high-resistance bulb that burned brightly for 170 hours.

"My light is perfected," Edison noted in his laboratory journal on November 28, 1879. He had done it. Now all he had to do was show the world.

Work for a public demonstration began immediately. Although no public announcement was made, news leaked out, and the simple farming village of Menlo Park became the center of the world's attention. People came by the trainloads to get a firsthand look at what they sensed was an historical achievement-in-progress. In the lab, Edison and his workers were tripping over visitors and giving tours explaining what they were doing.

Electric lights were clearly visible, being tested all

day and all night. Nevertheless, scientists around the world were doubtful, and experts in New York refused to visit. As one said, seeing the lamps would not prove how long they would last or how economical they would be. In London, John Tyndall, who had been working on the same problem, said that everyone knew that Edison's experiments were a "conspicuous failure."

Edison told a reporter from *The New York Times* that he was glad the experts weren't coming: "Practical men, with experience, and what I call 'horse sense' are the best judges of this light, and they are the men whom I like to welcome to my laboratory."

Meanwhile, lampposts were being erected around the hill on which Edison's lab sat. Underground wires were laid and connected to these poles and to a few other important buildings, such as Edison's house, his workshop, and the boardinghouse where several of his employees lived. Generators were built and the underground wires were connected to them. One bulb after another had to be made and tested, each one taking two men about six hours to produce. Over sixty bulbs were going to be needed for the gala event planned for midnight on New Year's Eve, 1879.

When the night arrived, there wasn't enough space on the trains for all the people who wanted to go to Menlo Park. Over 3,000 people crammed into the tiny village, as eager to see the new invention as they were to catch a glimpse of the thirty-two-year-old inventor.

Several times that evening, the switch was thrown and the circuit was closed. Each time, the thrilled crowds sent up a cheer. On the posts along the street, at the lab, at Edison's house, and at the boardinghouse, the lights came on in an instant and burned with a clean, steady glow. What they saw, Edison told his visitors, was nothing compared to what he was planning. Soon he was going to have 800 lights all around Menlo Park. After that he would light up the neighboring towns. Then he would move on to Newark, and then he would light all of New York City. "The sight," wrote one of Edison's employees, "was beautiful and in those days wonderful beyond belief."

10

City of Light

WHEN PRESIDENT RUTHERFORD B. Hayes decided against running for a second term in 1880, the conservative wing of the Republican Party began looking for a candidate who would bring back the "good old days." But a return to the past was the furthest thing from Thomas Edison's mind. Rather, at his lab in Menlo Park, the future was brewing. Thomas Edison was getting ready to take his electric bulb and make money from it. Before Edison began, electricity was produced by batteries and used mainly for telegraphs. When he was done, electricity was produced by generators and used in homes and factories all across the United States. With his new light, Edison ushered in the electric age.

On a hot Saturday night in August 1880, Edison boarded the train in Menlo Park. At Newark, he caught the Hudson River ferry, staying topside so that the river breeze could run through his hair and under his collar to cool him off a bit. It was around eleven o'clock at night when the boat docked. Edison walked off the wharf, up Broadway, and straight to the Bowery, where the nightlife was still going strong.

The Bowery was lined with nightclubs and restaurants that stayed open until nearly dawn. Out on the streets, throngs of people milled about, along with the pigs and dogs that roamed freely and the occasional dancing bear or monkey on a chain. There were even children out — young boys ready to run errands, trying to sell gum, candy, and flowers, and passing their free time playing tag or shooting dice in the avenue's alleys and doorways.

Edison often came into the city after his laboratory closed on Saturday evening, its one early closing day. He liked to walk around and take in a show before going over to Delmonico's, his favorite restaurant. But on this Saturday night he went straight to a three-story house on Wooster Street, just off the Bowery. Even though it was nearly midnight, Edison banged on the door until a man stuck his head out a top-floor window.

"Where's the fire?" the man shouted.

"Get dressed and come down," Edison yelled up to Sigmund Bergmann. "I want to speak to you."

Bergmann was happy to see Edison any time, day or night. He had worked for Edison in the early 1870s. When Edison had closed up his Newark shop, Bergmann opened a small electrical-equipment shop, and Edison soon became his most important customer. Since 1878, Bergmann had been manufacturing phonographs for the Edison Speaking Phonograph Company. Dressing quickly, he came downstairs, and the two men walked over to a small German restaurant where Edison gave Bergmann a quick rundown on what he had been doing.

Since the Menlo Park demonstrations, Edison had been busy perfecting the incandescent bulb. In the past few months, he had applied for more than twenty new bulb patents. He had set up a bulb-manufacturing plant in Menlo Park. He and his men had spent countless days and nights working on generators, wiring, and pipes for underground trenches. Rather than adding to the thick maze of wires that already blotted out the sky, it was Edison's idea to put electric wires underground. Charles Batchelor was going to produce the new generators from a plant on Goerck Street in Manhattan, once he got back from setting up some European demonstrations.

Lighting New York City was going to be a big job, Edison told Bergmann. The major pieces of his system were coming together, but he still needed someone to make small appliances. He already had several patents pending on devices such as sockets, switches, fixtures, meters, and safety fuses. Edison wanted Bergmann to manufacture them for him, and Bergmann was delighted to accommodate him.

He also needed the permission of New York City officials. This was at first difficult to obtain, owing to opposition from the rich and powerful heads of the gaslight companies. They feared that Edison's system might put them out of business, and used their influence with local politicians to keep Edison from getting started. Eventually, Edison so impressed city officials and business leaders with his demonstrations that he won the permission he needed.

In February 1881, a few days before his thirty-fourth birthday, Edison rented a brownstone at 65 Fifth Avenue in the fashionable Greenwich Village section of

New York. This brownstone was to be the business headquarters of the new company Edison had set up: Edison Electric Illuminating Company of New York. This company later became Consolidated Edison and is now known as Con Ed. It still supplies New York City with its electricity.

In what had been the back parlor of the house in Greenwich Village, Edison mounted a huge map, twelve feet high and fifteen feet wide. It showed every street and every building in a ten-block-by-ten-block district in New York's Wall Street area. This was where he would start. It was less impressive than lighting all of New York City, but Edison had to be reasonable. To light this area alone, they would have to dig fifteen miles of underground trenches.

Once the office was settled in New York, Edison got busy gathering information. He sent men into every shop and every office, asking how much gas was burned day and night. These facts were written on the map and used to figure out the size of the electric mains which would be placed in the underground trenches.

Edison's men started digging in December 1881, just before the winter frost made the ground rock hard. To keep the disruption to a minimum, the work went on only between eight in the evening and four in the morning. This meant that temporary lights and generators had to be trucked in each night. Edison himself supervised the setup, shouting directions over the bitter wind and making sure the cables stayed dry. Once everything was in place, one group of men started tearing up the cobblestones while another group dug the trench.

After the trenches were dug, the pipes had to be laid. Finding the best insulation to line these pipes and coat the wires had been a huge project in itself. Edison finally settled on a combination of asphalt, linseed oil, paraffin, and beeswax. Over on Washington Street, John Kruesi was supervising a group which was heating the insulation in huge vats. Strips of muslin were dipped into the hot mixture and then hand-wrapped around the wires as well as the inside each pipe. The smell was nauseating, and the neighbors were furious. But the work went on.

As each trench was dug and each pipe laid, Edison was right there, lifting and sweating and cursing with the rest of the men. He wanted to make sure every pipe was airtight and that every junction box was correctly placed. He worked until he could work no longer, and then he was likely to catch a nap on top of some pipes being stored at the power station he was building on Pearl Street. A few hours later, with new grease stains adorning his crumpled suit, Edison would be up and working once again. There were a thousand things to be done, and never enough time to do them.

After working all night in the trenches, Edison had to get over to his offices on Fifth Avenue to answer his mail, see to his bills, and give the orders for the day's work. Before long he would hear that he was needed on Goerck Street, where the generators were being built, or on Pearl Street, where the power station was being put together. Every few days he was forced to run out to Menlo Park, where the bulbs were being manufactured and where his family still lived.

When the cold weather really set in, all trench-work came to a halt. Edison had expected that. The stoppage didn't put him behind schedule. However, beginning in February 1882 there was an unexpected two-month break. Edison had to take time off to care for his wife. Mary, who turned twenty-seven in 1882, was not at all well. She had never really recovered from the birth of her son, Willie, in October 1878. By 1882, Mary weighed over 200 pounds and suffered from unbearable headaches and periods of terrible unhappiness.

"I think that an entire change would be of benefit," the Edison family doctor wrote to Tom about Mary. "She seems so changed physically and mentally of late that something ought to be done and I can suggest nothing better."

Since Mary liked Florida, Tom took her and the children down to Green Cove, a small town near St. Augustine. For the next two months, Mary got more attention from her husband than she usually got in two years. When she began to show improvement in April, Tom returned to New York.

Little had been accomplished while Edison was in Florida. Now he had to move forward, and fast. The newspapers knew all about what Edison was trying to do, and they were once again starting to write that Edison had promised the impossible. He was determined to prove them wrong.

Edison was soon working practically nonstop. Except for one night, he was back in the trenches, fighting to get the electric mains down. The one exception was when his men set the hands of his clock ahead six hours while Edison was napping. He woke up at 10 P.M., but by the clock thought it was four in the morning, time to knock off work. He sent everyone home and didn't realize what had happened until he saw the crowds exiting the theater as he was walking to his hotel room. Nearly an entire night's work lost!

During the day Edison tested systems and worked out bugs, all the while inventing new appliances. He took a big chance with one deal. This was a contract he made between Edison Lamp Works, in Menlo Park, and the Edison Electric Light Company, the company that had been set up to back Edison while he invented the bulb. Edison promised that his lamp company would sell the Electric Light Company all the bulbs they wanted for forty cents each. The Electric Light Company, which later became General Electric, thought Edison's offer was terrific. After all, each bulb cost much more than that to produce. For a while, it looked like Edison had worked his way into a financial dead end.

"The first year the lamps cost us about one dollar and ten cents each," Edison recalled. "We sold them for forty cents; but there were only about twenty or thirty thousand of them. The next year they cost us about seventy cents, and we sold them for forty. There were a good many, and we lost more money the second year than the first. The third year I succeeded in getting up machinery and in changing the processes, until it got down so that they cost somewhere around fifty cents. I still sold them for forty cents, and lost more money that year than any other because the sales were increasing rapidly. The fourth year I got it down to thirty-seven cents, and I made all the money in one year that I had lost previously. I finally got it down to twenty-two cents, and sold them for forty cents; and they were made by the million. Whereupon the Wall Street people thought it was a very lucrative business, so they concluded they would like to have it, and bought us out."

The incandescent bulb ended up making Edison a

rich man. In the meantime, the generator was tying his stomach in knots. It was spring 1882, and the generator was months behind schedule becasue Edison was having trouble making it powerful enough. With investors pressing him, and newspapers doubting his abilities, Edison announced that on Sunday, July 8, 1882, when downtown Manhattan was empty and quiet, he would run a full-scale test. He would throw the switch in the Pearl Street station to see how well the generator ran.

"At first everything worked all right," Edison said. But soon, the engines in the generator started seesawing. "One engine would stop and the other would run up to a thousand revolutions. Then the first engine would run up while the other stopped dead."

"It was a terrifying experience," said an observer. "The engines and dynamos [generators] made a horrible racket, and the place seemed to be filled with sparks and flames of all colors."

After this fiasco and the bad press that resulted, it seemed that most people had lost faith in Thomas Edison. He had made overblown claims about his inventions once too often. Edison also learned a painful lesson: He was better off avoiding publicity until he had finished all testing. He planned on connecting the generators to the rest of the system and starting it up by the end of the summer. But this time he didn't want the papers to know. The process was extremely complicated, and so much could go wrong.

September 4 was to be the big day. All through the day and night of September 3, Edison carefully rehearsed everyone's roles. He wanted to be sure everyone knew what to do if everything went smoothly as well as if — or rather *when* — a snag popped up.

Edison had invited only a few company directors to Pearl Street, and a couple of writers for scientific journals. Edison still didn't feel ready, but there was nothing more he could do. At midmorning on the fourth, he went back to 65 Fifth Avenue, changed into a Prince Albert coat, starched shirt, and derby hat, and went down to Pearl Street once again.

When Edison arrived, he may have looked relaxed on the outside, but on the inside he was very nervous. He was worn out. His stomach was in a knot, too, for he had been poisoning himself with too much chewing tobacco and too many cigars. One could say he was a wreck.

After explaining what was going to happen and then making a few last-minute checks, Edison finally gave the nod. At 3 o'clock in the afternoon on Monday, September 4, 1882, he ordered one generator engine turned on. He didn't dare run more than one; he couldn't take a chance that they would seesaw as they had in July.

The switch was pulled, and the generator sputtered to life. For the first time in history, current flowed from a commercial power station, through underground mains, into stores and offices, and into Edison's incandescent bulbs. The bulbs may have looked dim in the strong afternoon sun, but the system worked.

Hidden on an inside page, as if it weren't very important, the *New York World* reported the next morning that "most of the principal stores from Fulton and Nassau Street were lighted by electricity for the first time." *The New York Times* wrote, "It was not until about 7 o'clock, when it began to be dark, that the electric light really made itself known."

New York took the event calmly, probably because

Edison had cried wolf once too often. But this time, when Edison gave the order to set the power flowing, he had really done it. He had accomplished far more than lighting up a few buildings. He had done more than deliver a working incandescent bulb. He had figured out how to tame a powerful new source of energy. When he pulled that switch, Thomas Alva Edison had brought the world into the age of electricity.

"I have accomplished all that I promised," said an exhausted Edison with a sigh of relief.

11

The Middle Years

IN AUGUST 1884, a worried Thomas Edison, thirty-seven years old, chewed a wad of tobacco and paced the front porch of his house in Menlo Park. His hands were behind his back and his eyes were on his feet. In the last five years, he had been so occupied with his many businesses and his new base in New York that he hadn't spent much time in Menlo Park. When he lifted his head to spit tobacco juice over the porch rail, Edison couldn't help but notice that a lot had changed.

The wood-plank walkway at his front step no longer led to a bustling laboratory. The lab was closed and empty. The locomotive of an electric train, an invention Edison started working on in his spare time in 1880, sat abandoned in the knee-high weeds outside the now-silent machine shop. Every time he looked at that locomotive, Edison was reminded of the wild rides he and his lab workers had enjoyed. But the railroad tracks had been torn up and sold. The assistants had scattered, working in Edison businesses around the country and around the world.

Menlo Park no longer dazzled the world with its electric lights. The town had been a terrific site for demonstrating Edison's wonderful new achievement. But it would be years before the town would be wired in earnest. The lampposts, underground wires, and sockets remained, as did the electric chandeliers in Edison's house. But they were useless — shells of their former selves. The generators that had pumped life into them had long since been removed. In five years, Menlo Park had reverted from the technological center of the world into a sleepy, farming village where people rocked on their front porches, swishing away flies in the dense summer heat.

While Edison was lighting up New York City, his family had left Menlo Park to join him. Edison bought an elegant house on Gramercy Park, where he and his family lived quite fashionably. After Tom threw the switch in September 1882 and lit the Wall Street area, all the Edisons stayed on in New York. From his headquarters at 65 Fifth Avenue, Tom was running several businesses and trying to sell his system to other cities. Meanwhile, he was using his small laboratory on Goerck Street to make improvements and new inventions. Mary stayed in New York because she was busier and less lonely there. She and the children usually escaped the winter cold by going to Florida. During the summer, they took advantage of the breezes at the nearby Jersey shore.

August 1884, however, was different. Mary and the children — eleven-year-old Marion (Dot), eight-year-old Thomas Jr. (Dash), and five-year-old William — had been in Menlo Park for over four months. Despite the heat, Mary had not taken her children to the shore, for she was in no condition to travel. Suffering from violently painful headaches, she was unable to take care of her children, her home, or even herself. Mary was deathly ill.

Tom had three doctors and a male nurse taking care of Mary that summer. The headaches and dizziness had grown much worse. At times she became completely irrational and had to be restrained. That was the reason for the male nurse. A female would have been unable to hold back a struggling woman weighing well over 200 pounds.

As August 8, 1884, drew to a close, Tom was at Mary's bedside. She was hot and sweaty. Tom wiped her brow with a damp cloth. She complained that her throat felt parched and sore. He gave her something to drink. But there was nothing he could do for her painful headache.

In the early hours of August 9, Dot Edison was awakened by the sounds of her father's sobbing. "I found him shaking with grief, weeping and sobbing so he could hardly tell me that mother had died in the night," she later recalled.

Years later, when Dot asked her father how her mother died, he told her that Mary had died of typhoid fever. In fact, it is more likely that Mary Edison died of a brain tumor, but that was something Edison had trouble accepting. His mind, after all, was his greatest asset. Once, while tapping his forehead, he commented that creditors could never get his factory, no matter what. To Edison, an illness that affected the mind was a blot on his family, and so he denied it.

Mary Stilwell Edison was only twenty-nine years old when she died. She left her husband with three young children to raise, three children that he barely knew. Although Edison loved them, sometimes invented toys for them, and occasionally even played with them, he was basically a distant father. Edison didn't know what to do with his two young boys. Most of the time he left them with Mary's mother, who ran his household for him. Whenever he could, he also sent them off to his brother, Pitt, or to his sister, Marion, both of whom were living in Ohio. Edison had no idea that his sons would suffer, feeling rejected and unloved for the rest of their lives.

At the same time, he delighted in his daughter. She was enrolled in Madame Mears's Madison Avenue French Academy, a private girl's school. But Edison kept her with him at home much of the time. All through the fall of 1884 and the following winter and spring, Dot was her father's favored companion. Exhausted from the superhuman efforts of the last six years, Edison for once decided to take it easy. With Dot at his side, he went to various business meetings, checked out how things were going on Pearl Street, and went over to the Goerck Street laboratory. In the evening he liked to take Dot to the opera, where they sat up close and Edison cupped his hand behind an ear so that he could catch some of the music. They usually ended up with dinner in the men's dining room at Delmonico's. It was common for the twelve-year-old Dot to stay out until midnight and later.

In the summer of 1885, while the boys were in Ohio, Edison took Dot out to Menlo Park for a visit. Mary's sister, Alice, was living in the Edison's house with her husband, William Holzer. They were trying to raise chickens on the old laboratory grounds. In a diary he

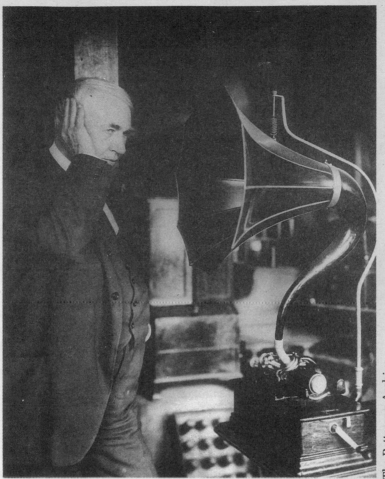

Edison with an updated 1911-model phonograph, vastly different from the one he had created as a young man. Ironically, the man who had so much to do with sound recordings was hard of hearing since childhood.

kept for a short while, Edison wrote of sitting on the porch one day after a family lunch. After an afternoon buggy ride and an early supper, Dot somehow convinced her father to go out on the lawn and throw a ball around with her. In all his thirty-eight years, this was the first time Edison had ever played catch. After a few minutes he smashed his little finger into the ball and swore off the game for the next thirty-eight years.

At sundown, Edison went inside to read by the light of a gas lamp. It would be another quarter of a century before anyone in Menlo Park, the birthplace of the electric light, would be able to read by one of Edison's bulbs. But that didn't stop Edison. He had an endless appetite for books, which he bought by the shelf and had shipped home in crates. Although he liked all kinds of reading, on that July evening in 1885 he chose the *Encyclopedia Britannica.* He needed, he claimed, something "to steady my nerves." After such a relaxing day, one would hardly think he needed to rest, but his nerves weren't the real problem. It was his heart, which ached with longing every time he thought about a young woman named Mina Miller. Thomas Edison had fallen in love.

Mina Miller was the daughter of a wealthy Midwestern manufacturer. Edison first met her in February 1885 at an industrial fair in New Orleans, Louisiana. Tom, who had just turned thirty-eight, didn't make much of an impression on the slim, clever, black-haired twenty-year-old. She already had a suitor, a man much closer in age to herself. Unlike Edison, this young man was well-groomed, well-spoken, and well-liked by her parents.

Four months later, Edison saw Mina Miller again at

Lillian and Ezra Gilliland's house in Boston. The Gillilands knew Mina through her father, and Tom and Ezra had been friends and business associates ever since Tom was a young telegrapher. Ezra and his wife invited both Tom and Mina to a dinner party, where Mina's piano playing and singing made a deep impression. "I could not help being interested immediately," Edison wrote in his diary that night, "in anyone who would play and sing without hesitation, when they did it as bad as that."

That summer the Gillilands arranged several other house parties at their vacation home in Woodside, Massachusetts. Tom and Dot were usually there because, by this time, Tom was completely under Mina's spell. Mina, for her part, had become interested in Tom as well. Since Edison didn't want the other houseguests to hear him trying to win Mina's heart, he taught her Morse code during the hot summer afternoons. After that, they held long private talks, even when they were surrounded by others, tapping out the code on each other's hands. It was during one of these "talks" that Tom proposed. Mina accepted.

The wedding was a grand affair held at the Miller's mansion in Akron, Ohio, on February 24, 1886. Hundreds of people came to see the wedding procession march down a bright red carpet spread on the lawn and ending under a giant bell of roses. After the wedding the newlyweds spent two months in Fort Meyers, Florida, where Tom had bought land and was having a winter home built. At the end of April, Tom and Mina went back north to West Orange, New Jersey, to move into a rambling mansion called Glenmont.

It wasn't long before the Edison family settled into life

at Glenmont. The boys, Tom Jr. and Will, were sent off to boarding school. Dot, who had trouble getting along with her new stepmother, first went to boarding school and later to Europe. Edison plunged eagerly into his work. To Mina's surprise, her husband's attentiveness ended after their honeymoon. She had expected, at the least, a little conversation at the breakfast table. What she got was a view of the back page of *The New York Times*. Like Mary before her, Mina was left alone most of the time to figure out what to do with her life besides caring for the three children she bore: Madeline, Charles, and Theodore, born in 1888, 1890, and 1898, respectively.

One of the things Mina came to do was entertain. Glenmont, with its sprawling lawns and massive shade trees, its receiving rooms, libraries, and large parlors, was the perfect setting. Under Mina's direction, great people gathered at Glenmont. Scientists, industrialists, governors, and even presidents accepted her invitations even though Mina could never be certain whether Tom would leave his work to join them.

While Mina orchestrated the Edisons' social life, Tom fashioned what many came to call the Age of Edison. Between the late 1880s and the early 1900s, his electric system slowly caught on all across the United States, changing the way people lived and worked. His generator was the basis of the engines that powered American industries. His phonograph became a common addition to American homes. But to Edison these were all *old* inventions, and Edison's inventiveness was still going strong.

Near Glenmont, in West Orange, he built another commercial-research laboratory, even bigger than the

Menlo Park lab, and the inventions kept pouring out. Although he may be best remembered for the electric light, in the upcoming years Edison would make significant contributions to mining, plastics, chemistry, and many other fields of science and industry.

Edison's first major project was the magnetic ore-separator. His separator crushed low-grade iron-ore — deposits that were considered worthless — and pulled out the iron with magnets. Edison had grand plans for this invention. He sent men out all over the country, searching for deposits and buying up mineral rights. He planned to sell these rights to companies that bought his separator. He also poured millions into an ore-separator plant in Ogdensburg, New Jersey. But this idea never worked out. The machinery created billows of dust, choking the workers and clogging the equipment. In addition, the processed iron wasn't pure enough. The final blow came in late 1899, when cheap high-grade iron-ore was discovered and started being mined in Minnesota, putting Edison out of business.

Much of the testing and reworking of the ore-separator had been done on full-scale machines at Ogdensburg. But during those same years, Edison was also busy with other projects back in West Orange. In 1889 Edison could often be found in one of his four laboratory buildings, experimenting with a new storage battery. When he wasn't there, he was sitting in a haze of cigar smoke while thinking through problems in his wood-paneled office. This bright room had a massive fireplace along one wall and photographs and portraits of himself and other famous people mounted all about. It was located in the middle of a three-story library that was larger than most small colleges had at the time. In an alcove downstairs near Tom's desk, Mina had installed a bed. Now, when Edison worked all night, he didn't have to curl up on a worktable to catch a few hours' sleep.

The alkaline-storage battery was one of Edison's most successful inventions. It was used for train signals, radios, miners' lamps, and hundreds of other things. But what Edison originally had in mind was an electric car, since he had always hated horses. A few electric cars were built with Edison storage batteries, but they were expensive and slow. Cars with gasoline engines were more popular, even though early models belched and bucked and had to be started with a crank. Henry Ford, the car manufacturer who revolutionized factory methods by creating the assembly line, asked Edison to solve the problem of hand-cranked starts in 1911 by inventing a battery-powered starting system. Edison never made the starting system, but this marked the beginning of a deep and long-lasting friendship between Edison and Ford.

One of the most popular inventions to come out of West Orange started as an idea Edison had in 1887 for matching moving pictures to the phonograph's sound. "The idea occurred to me," Edison wrote in his diary, "that it was possible to devise an instrument which would do for the eye what the phonograph does for the ear, and that by a combination of the two all motion and sound could be recorded and reproduced simultaneously."

Edison was unable to match up motion with sound, but he did invent the kinetoscope, a camera that could take motion pictures. America's movie industry was born not in Hollywood, California, but in the moving-picture studio Edison built outside his West Orange laboratories. For many years, almost all movies were made and filmed in New Jersey.

Edison believed that movies should be used to educate, but as always financial considerations affected his output. From 1893 to 1894, the "educational" films Edison made included all sorts of circus performers, both human and animal. Then, in 1894, Edison discovered that the public had a taste for boxing exhibitions. Over the next few years he satisfied that taste by filming scores of matches — real prizefights as well as phony ones — and made a great deal of money renting these and other one-reel scenes to the film parlors that were popping up all over the country. It wasn't until 1904 that a movie was made that told a complete story. In the woods and meadows outside of West Orange, Edison's assistant, William Dickson, directed the first western. It was called *The Great Train Robbery*. Edison subsequently lost interest in movies. After all, Edison wrote in his diary, "I was an inventor — an experimenter. I wasn't a theatrical producer."

In 1914, Thomas Edison turned sixty-seven years old. Many of the people he knew and loved had died, including his brother, Pitt, his father, Sam, and his sister, Marion. In 1899, John Kruesi had died, at age fifty-six, after working for Edison for thirty years. Charles Batchelor had died in 1910. Through everything, Edison submerged himself in work. In the early 1900s, that work had included improving the phonograph and inventing a dictating machine. In 1914, when the source of the carbolic acid he used for phonograph records was threatened by growing hostilities between the countries of Europe, Edison devised a method of making carbolic acid from benzol and then built a plant for synthesizing carbolic acid. By 1915, World War I had broken out and his source of benzol was gone. Working day and night for forty-five days, he engineered and built his own benzol plant. Immediately afterward, he built plants for textile chemicals also unavailable because of the war.

In 1916, before the United States entered World War I, Edison created the Naval Research Laboratory. There he invented submarine-defense systems, antisubmarine devices, and other naval equipment. Unfortunately, almost none of his ideas were used, even though he worked through the war. The large Navy bureaucracy prevented things from happening as quickly as Edison was accustomed to.

Edison worked on through the 1920s and his own failing health. In 1929, at age eighty-two the owner of over 1,000 patents, more than any inventor before or since, Edison was actively trying to figure out how to make rubber from local plants. In October of that year, a week before the stock market on Wall Street crashed and the Great Depression began, Tom and Mina Edison traveled to Dearborn, Michigan, where his friend Henry Ford had built a replica of Menlo Park. It had been fifty years since Edison had invented the light bulb, and Ford had organized a golden jubilee for the event.

12

A Career to Celebrate

IT WAS OCTOBER 21, 1929. An eighty-two-year-old, white-haired Thomas Edison stood stoop-shouldered outside a picket fence. Nearby stood his wife, Mina, and two of his friends, Henry Ford, the owner of the Ford Motor Company, and Harvey Firestone, the owner of the Firestone Tire & Rubber Company. They were watching Edison as he looked over the fence into what appeared to be his old Menlo Park laboratory grounds. Only this wasn't Menlo Park. It was Dearborn, Michigan. Henry Ford had built an historic recreation of Menlo Park, a monument to Thomas Edison and his work.

"I can't believe it," Edison said. He had been ailing for the last few years, plagued with stomach problems. But as he looked at the place where he had been happiest and most productive, Edison began to stand up straighter and look younger. Mina, beside him, became worried and began fussing with his coat, trying to button him up. Tom brushed her aside impatiently.

"I'm all right," he said. "I'm just as young as I was

when I worked there in the old laboratory." Sighing, Mina left him alone.

"I can't believe it," Edison repeated. "Look there," he said to Harvey Firestone. "There's the old boarding-house, just like it looked. And by golly if Henry hasn't even moved in the stump of that old elm tree. I tell you, it's just exactly as it was, every last bit of it." Opening the gate and walking inside, Edison kicked the dirt with his shoe and laughed. "Why, Henry's even got the damn New Jersey clay here."

Slowly, painfully, Edison lumbered up the walk, into the building, and up the stairs to see his old lab once more. When he walked in the door, he stopped.

"It's amazing. Truly amazing," he said quietly as he walked, alone now, into the room and sat in an old wooden chair. It was all there. There was the table where he and Batchelor and Adams had worked out the designs for the first phonograph. In the middle of the room was the vacuum pump whose clanging and thumping had tortured everyone when those first experimental light bulbs were being made. At the back of the room was the pipe organ where the men would gather after their midnight dinner to relax and sing.

While Edison sat, lost in his memories, no one moved or spoke. They all waited. Finally he got up, turned to Henry Ford, and yelled out, "Well, you've got this just about ninety-nine and one-half percent perfect."

Ford had spent years putting this museum together. He had scoured the New Jersey countryside collecting doors and furniture and hardware from the original buildings. He had excavated a garbage pit where Edison and his workers had tossed old and broken equipment. He had even glued together, piece by piece, a ceramic mortar and pestle that Edison used to use to grind chemicals to powder. After all that, why was it only ninety-nine and one-half percent perfect?

"What is the matter with the other one-half percent?" Ford wanted to know.

"Well," Edison answered, chuckling a little, "We never kept it as clean as this."

The Dearborn museum showed Menlo Park as it was on October 21, 1879. That was the day when Edison had overcome the last and biggest stumbling block to inventing a working light bulb. He had finally tested a carbon filament with high electrical resistance. Exactly fifty years later, Henry Ford's golden jubilee celebrated that invention. On the evening of October 21, 1929, when the sun went down, there was to be a reenact ment of the test of the first working bulb, followed by a dramatization of the lighting of Menlo Park.

The evening was rainy and chilly. Mina worried about Tom as they left a dinner that was held in his honor and returned to the lab for the ceremonies. Once again they climbed the stairs to the upstairs lab. This time President Herbert Hoover and his wife had joined the group standing just inside the doorway watching Edison. The room was dimly lit, as it would have looked by gas lamp. But the view outside the tall laboratory windows was nothing like what Edison had seen in 1879. Instead of the dark, rural New Jersey country-side, Henry Ford's automobile factory was framed by the windows. The lights were on, and smoke was rising from the chimneys.

The view of that factory showed how much Thomas Edison had changed the world. There would never have been such a factory without Thomas Edison's inventions. Without the electric starters made possible by his storage battery, cars would never have become so popular. Edison had introduced the electric generator, which was the basis of the engines that run factories. Even more important, it was Thomas Edison who had figured out how to control and harness electricity, the power that drives the factory engines. Finally, Thomas Edison invented the electric light, making it possible to stretch the day into the night and keep that factory beyond the window operating. Thomas Alva Edison's inventions had brought the world into the modern age. In a real sense, he invented modern America.

Upstairs, in his re-created laboratory, Edison shuffled slowly over to the worktable. His stomach was bothering him, and he was exhausted, but it must have been a moment of triumph. As he sat at the table, an old-fashioned, hand-blown bulb was brought over to him. The wires were placed inside, and then the bulb was brought over to the vacuum pump. While the air was being pumped out of the bulb, an orchestra outside played "Oh, Susanna." Radio reporters were scattered throughout the room talking into their microphones, and newspaper reporters were taking notes. The event was being shared by the world. Finally the pumping stopped.

"The lamp has a good vacuum," said Francis Jehl, one of the few Menlo Park assistants still alive.

"Seal it," Edison ordered.

As Edison prepared to test the bulb, a radio announcer built up the suspense. "It is now ready for the critical test," he said quietly. "Will it light? Will it burn?"

Edison turned the switch. "Ladies and gentlemen, it lights," the announcer said. Thousands of lights were then turned on throughout the recreated village. A bell in a replica of Independence Hall began to ring. As airplanes circled the village and fireworks were shot off, the announcer continued: "Light's golden jubilee has come to a triumphant climax."

Meanwhile, Thomas Edison returned to the celebration dinner. When he arrived, he sank into a couch just outside the dining room. He was totally drained and pale.

"I won't go in," Edison said to Mina. "I can't go in."

After several minutes of pleading and coaxing, Mina was able to convince him to go inside. She didn't want him to disappoint the hundreds of people in the hall and the millions eagerly listening in at their radios. They were all waiting to hear Edison speak. But his exhaustion ran deep. Edison managed to read through his speech, after which he stayed, slumped in his chair, through the speeches given in his honor. But he heard none of them. When he went home after this celebration, he was never again strong enough to go back to his full work schedule.

Edison had driven himself hard all his life. His usual workday had been sixteen to eighteen hours. Sometimes he worked around the clock. He smoked too much and chewed too much tobacco. For the last few years he had been living on nothing but milk. This was after spending years eating little besides coffee and pie. Despite everything, he had lived to be eighty-two. But he was worn out.

Almost two years later, on August 1, 1931, Thomas Alva Edison collapsed at his home. Two months after that he sank into a coma. He died quietly in his bed in Glenmont during the early morning hours of Sunday, October 18, 1931. He was eighty-four years old.

The funeral was held on Wednesday, October 21. At ten o'clock that night, eastern standard time, lights were dimmed all across the United States in Edison's memory. Motion pictures stopped, New York City's Great White Way on Broadway was turned off, theater spotlights were blacked out, and the Statue of Liberty's torch was extinguished. Subway trains were also stopped, honoring Edison's invention of the electric train.

But many more things could have stopped that night. Telephones could have been disconnected. Without Edison's improvements, the telephone had been useless. Radios could have been blacked out, for he discovered radio waves. Automobile traffic could have been halted, because he had been responsible for the car's storage battery. In fact, our whole way of life could have ground to a halt.

"Few inventors succeeded in transforming society as Edison did in his own lifetime," wrote a *New York Times* editor. "He found a world burning kerosene and gas; he left it viewing motion pictures, painting with his electric lights and listening to his phonograph. . . . This electrical age is his creation."

Other books you might enjoy reading

1. Conot, Robert. *A Streak of Luck.* Da Capo Press, 1986.

2. Edison, Thomas Alva. *The Diary and Observations of Thomas Alva Edison.* Philosophical Library, 1976.

3. Ford, Henry, *Edison as I Know Him.* Cosmopolitan Book Company, 1930.

4. Frost, Lawrence A. *The Edison Album; A Pictorial Biography of Thomas Alva Edison.* Superior Publishing Company, 1969.

5. Hutchings, David W. *Edison at Work.* Hastings House, 1969.

6. Meadowcroft, William Henry, *The Boy's Life of Edison.* Harper & Row, 1949.

ABOUT THE AUTHOR

Penny Mintz is the author of *The Cholesterol Counter* (Ballantine) and *The New Year's Shape Up* (Price Stern Sloan), and her articles have appeared in *The New York Times, Newsday, New York, Newsweek,* and other publications. She was for many years an editor of elementary and high-school textbooks. She lives in New York City with her husband and two children.